From the

ERRORS

of Others

What others are saying...

"Rebecca Lyles's *From the Errors of Others* is the most helpful and engaging book on English I've ever read. It is also brilliantly entertaining. As the author suggests, English is a funny language. But you have no idea *how* funny until you read this informative book. Errors in English are like ink spots on your face. People stare at them and wonder about you. Lyles helps you avoid the errors. So, if you're in business, in school, in a job interview, in a cocktail party—or writing a presentation, a speech, a love letter—or if you just need some belly laughs, it would be an *Error* to not read this book!"
— *Mike Brogan, award-winning novelist, Madison's Avenue, G8, Dead Air, Business to Kill For*

"I was lucky to have Rebecca as my boss and mentor at two companies, and she helped make me the writer I am today. Now you can benefit from Rebecca's wisdom and realize how lucky you are to have this book."
— *Eric Bütow, computer book author for Que, Wiley, and more*

"*From the Errors of Others* is an excellent book to own if you value the skill of writing. You can open the book to any page and start enjoying Ms. Lyles's sense of humor and witty style.

Through her amusing anecdotes, you learn to avoid the same mistakes that have claimed the egos of those who wrote before you."

— *Jonathan Fales, Senior course developer, IBM ECM Education*

"Rebecca has a special way of drawing your attention to writing and speaking errors in a fun and informative way. I highly recommend this book to anyone looking to improve their communication skills in their personal and professional life."

— *Eric Vonheim, Manager at IBM and Professor at Santa Ana College*

"After you stop laughing at your colleagues' mistakes, take a good look at that speech you were going to give or that slide show you have to present and take Ms. Lyles's lessons to heart. Your audience will thank you."

— *Virginia Janzig, Technical Editor, IBM ECM Education (Ret.)*

"Rebecca has been my personal Grammar Checker for years. I once questioned her pronunciation of "primer," as in a 1st grade primer. She very politely explained that my own pronunciation referred to car paint. Oops! To avoid embarrassing errors in your business and personal communications, use this book. It is a great primer."

— *Jean Munday, MS Systems Management, University of Southern California*

From the——
ERRORS
——of Others

How to Avoid
Embarrassing
Mistakes
in Writing
and Speaking

REBECCA M. LYLES

ARCHWAY
PUBLISHING

Archway Publishing books may be ordered through booksellers or by contacting:

Archway Publishing
1663 Liberty Drive
Bloomington, IN 47403
www.archwaypublishing.com
1 (888) 242-5904

ISBN: 978-1-4808-2846-9 (sc)
ISBN: 978-1-4808-2847-6 (hc)
ISBN: 978-1-4808-2848-3 (e)

Library of Congress Control Number: 2016907295

Print information available on the last page.

Archway Publishing rev. date: 5/24/2016

Dedication

To Georgia Moore
I'm sorry I never thanked you.

Miss Moore had a long career in a bygone era as a small-town high school teacher of English and Literature. With uncommon intelligence and dignity, she inspired countless ragamuffins who became lawyers, professors, healers, cartoonists, executives, authors, free thinkers, lifelong readers, and otherwise generally literate adults. We went off to college, and then we scattered ourselves around the globe, pursuing bigger lives than hers without ever looking back. By the time it occurred to most of us to tell her how much she'd meant to us, she was gone.

If you know a Georgia Moore, tell her today.

Introduction

"From the errors of others..."

Publilius Syrus, I'm told, was a Roman slave in the first century BC. Intelligent and clever, he was obviously over-qualified for the job. Details are sketchy, but it seems he gained his freedom and eventually earned respect for his plays and theatrical performances. His pithy sayings have inspired centuries of luminaries, including William Shakespeare, who allegedly managed to work them into his own writings.

As I searched for a short phrase that would sum up the message in this book, one of Syrus's gems stood out from the rest. I worried that all my attention to writing mistakes and speaking blunders would come across as negative or condescending. But, centuries ago, Syrus put the responsibility right where it belongs and gave people a choice. No one ever said you *must* be a wise person. Even our Founding Fathers, God bless 'em, gave us the freedom to be classless idiots if that's what we wanted to be. It follows that anyone who admires the Horrible Examples in this book is free to adopt them rather than learn from them. I hope you don't, but—just so you know—it's still a free country.

Most articulate communicators did not learn their skills by taking a few courses. Formal instruction teaches you the basics and, if you remember them, provides a foundation for lifelong learning. But effective communication is a complex, situational, and ever-changing pursuit in which perfection is impossible. Experts disagree, rules change, and your audience often dictates what's appropriate and what's not. The best we can do is to do the best we can.

Word choices and expressions can be intensely personal. They define who you are. They shape the perceptions other people have about you. Some situations require you to decide in a split second, "Do I want to seem ignorant to smart people or condescending to ignorant people?" As communication goes through a Great Dumbing Down process, must you bend to meet the masses? And if you join them, what will smart people think of you? Hiring managers, clients, sales prospects, friends and co-workers, potential romantic partners?

Be of good cheer. In most cases, you don't have to choose between option A and option B. If neither feels comfortable, there's usually an option C.

This is not a grammar book. The opinions expressed are mine, so it is useless to engage me in a debate over fine points, arguments for prescriptive or descriptive approaches, or how many angels can dance on the head of a pin. I split infinitives, end sentences with prepositions, and write incomplete sentences. All the time. So please don't send me hate mail. This book is about what works in the business world, dealing with the public, and in personal and social situations.

From the Errors of Others is a collection of short essays, most including observations and true anecdotes about awkward—often funny—gaffes and missteps I've experienced. Under the cloak of anonymity and in the comfort of your own home, you can laugh *about* the guilty without laughing *at* them, and make mental notes to avoid repeating their mistakes. Read it in any order you like, skip around, put it down and pick it up again. Each essay contains a small lesson to help you improve the way you write or speak.

Errors. We all make them. And from the errors of others, as Publilius Syrus said,

"…a wise man corrects his own."

Rebecca Lyles

Contents

—————————All Business

Picture yourself outside a business looking in, struggling to impress with résumés, profiles, job interviews, and online listings. It's natural for job seekers to want every advantage they can find.

How do I get their attention? Should I pay for conflicting advice on the best way to get a foot in the door? Is this a good font for my résumé? How about the paper? Ivory? Gray? White? Please, I hope you think I'm pretty enough to join your sorority.

None of that matters, of course, because many résumés are accepted online or are scanned into databases. The hiring manager probably never sees the original. The part that does matter is the content. And what about your online profile? Your Internet presence (LinkedIn, Facebook, your personal website) is easy to overlook, but it needs to be as squeaky-clean as the résumé. Everything you post online is potentially visible to a hiring manager.

Now picture yourself inside, looking out. Companies are always scrambling to influence customers, employees, potential employees, and investors. Marketing departments and ad agencies obsess over how to project the most positive image and beat the competition. Everything—from the name on the building to the message that telephone customers hear when they're placed on hold—is important in crafting this image. And yet, business communication seems either full of frantic hype or dull to the point of anesthesia.

One culprit is the tired, meaningless jargon that passes for business language. Sales and Marketing are to blame for much of it, and few companies are immune. When you read a sentence packed with *utilize, leverage, solutions, capabilities, functionality, issues, perspectives,* and *paradigms*, it's like eating empty calories. Cotton candy words—noise with no substance. Add a few passive verbs and you have cellulose with no nutritional value whatsoever.

Styles vary with the type and size of the company, but many communications fail because the senders didn't give enough thought to how the audience might receive them. This is why some companies pay big bucks for market research and targeted advertising. But then they conduct surveys and ignore the results. They train their customer-facing employees to be annoyingly cheerful and give them scripts to read.

For job seekers and job providers alike, the best start is to imagine yourself in the audience. What does this person or company really want? If you can do that, you're already ahead of the competition. If you can't or won't, you'll end up in the alley outside a locked door, wondering what on earth went wrong.

Three Common
——————————— Profile Mistakes

Your career profile on LinkedIn, your website, or your Facebook business page needs to give a quick overview of your skills and accomplishments. Busy people have short attention spans. So if you're trying to attract clients, investors, or potential employers, the profile is your fifteen-second opportunity to grab their attention. Most of all, you want to avoid anything that makes the reader stop reading.

We'll start by assuming you know that vague, overblown claims are useless. Phrases such as *various worldwide leadership roles* and *global impact on society* tell the reader nothing about what you can do or what you have done. Buzzwords and clichés sound like exactly what they are—filler. If your profile is loaded with these, rewrite it using more concrete evidence of your achievements.

Your profile sums up your potential value to readers. It's all right to paint an honest, positive picture of yourself. Go ahead and tell your story, taking whatever credit you deserve for all you've done. But if you claim *too* much credit, remember that whoever really did the work might be reading it.

Make sure the facts you cite are related to what you actually contributed. It's not impressive to claim, "I swept floors at a company headquarters building valued at seventy million dollars." If you designed, built, or decorated it, that's another matter.

Once your profile is tight, specific, and compelling, check for these common errors.

- ## Principle or principal

Are you a founder or major figure in a company? Then you're a *principal*, not a principle. If your title is something like Principal Member of Technical Team, spell it right. Nothing erodes confidence more quickly than misspelling your own title. Would you trust someone who claimed to be a Doctor of Filosofy?

- ## Lead or led

Describe your past experience in the past tense. Say you *sold, managed, developed, supervised, delivered,* or *led*—not lead—something. The past tense of *lead* is *led*. *Lead*—pronounced "leed"— is present tense, and it means you're still doing that job. *Lead*—pronounced "led"—is a soft, malleable metal.

- ## Writing in third person

Your profile is about you, and everyone knows you wrote it. It's no secret, and no one expects it to read like a newspaper article written by someone else. People who write in third person seem to think it gives them license to brag about themselves without seeming immodest. In fact, it has the opposite effect. It seems disingenuous and awkward. If your experience and skills are strong, the facts speak for themselves without hype or pretense. Save third person for recommendations, when you are writing about someone else.

Cautionary tale—Years ago, a member of my university's newspaper staff wrote a shamelessly self-serving article about herself. Her name was in the headline and in nearly every sentence of the article. She intended it to run with no byline, as if it were a genuine news piece. But the editor was so tired of her relentless self-promotion that he sent it to press with her name under the headline, credited as the writer. The next day, twenty thousand students enjoyed a great front-page laugh with their morning coffee—at her expense. Oops.

Advice about Revenge and Duplicity

In the classic film *The Princess Bride*, Inigo Montoya seeks *revenge* on an elusive villain. The master swordsman repeats throughout the movie, "Hello. My name is Inigo Montoya. You killed my father. Prepare to die."

In another movie, *The Avengers*, superheroes seek retribution for—they *avenge*—crimes against others.

Revenge is a noun.

Avenge is a verb.

I wonder, then, why there is such an epidemic of writing like this:

- The grieving mother has sworn to *revenge* the wrongful death of her son...

- Our foreign policy was intended to *revenge* the military actions of...

- What would you have done to *revenge* 9/11?

To *avenge* something is to seek *revenge*. The words are not interchangeable.

Mother's Day brings out a flood of tributes to moms who always gave good *advise*.

> *Advice* is a noun.

> *Advise* is a verb.

Mom gave good *advice*. To *advise* someone is to give *advice*. The words are not interchangeable.

Those two examples are at least related in meaning, and there is some weak justification for the confusion. But this one is inexplicable:

"I have two versions of my résumé, and there is a lot of *duplicity* between them."

> *Duplication* means repeated content.

> *Duplicity* means deception.

Within a single version of your résumé, *duplication* makes it wordy. And two versions of your résumé might highlight different skills but contain the same basic information, a necessary *duplication*. The difference is that *duplicity* suggests double-dealing or deceitfulness. People with *duplicity* in their résumés are not likely to admit it.

When job seekers ask my *advice,* I *advise* them to avoid both *duplication* and *duplicity.* If you lie to get a job, your manager will *avenge* the act and exact this *revenge*: "Hello. I am your boss. You lied on your résumé. Prepare to be unemployed."

————————— What Are You, Five?

This is about childish expressions, and that title is an example of one. Many childish phrases are argumentative and confrontational, so we'll just avoid those. I'm assuming if you're old enough to read this, you no longer engage in such playground banter as, "Sez who?" "Oh yeah?" and "None of your beeswax."

But even if you do, there's a difference between using these words playfully in speech and using them in writing or in a business context. Thank goodness, many companies still prefer to hire grown-ups who talk like grown-ups.

The one that makes my teeth ache is *on accident*. Most children were corrected by their elementary school teachers and taught to say "by accident" instead. But a few people—maybe they were absent that day—failed to retain this lesson beyond second grade.

I'm not sure when this one crept into adult conversation, but when I hear *for realz*, I wonder if the speaker is secretly that Internet cat who luvz him some cheezburgers. And what about referring to everyone, regardless of gender, as *you guys*? I once dated a guy who, when a perky beverage server asked, "Hi! What can I get for you guys?" replied mock-conspiratorially, "One of us is not a guy, but bring a chardonnay for the lady, and I'll have a Sam Adams."

Lest you think I'm singling out young people again, I continue to see e-mails and texts from senior citizens who, though they are to be commended for embracing technology, have picked up the bad spelling habits of texters and tweeters. I refuse to take seriously any message containing *cuz* for *because*. If used as an affectionate nickname for one's cousin, that's different.

I understand why, at lunch or in a meeting, someone would not want to announce, "I have to use the toilet," or the equally offensive, "I need a bio break." Crude. But, really, do we have to say, "I'm going to the little boys' (or little girls') room?" I always picture a nursery school restroom with teeny-tiny facilities. What's wrong with just, "Excuse me"?

Different situations call for different communication styles, and successful communication demands good judgment about the style you choose. If you were considering someone for a business promotion, how would you feel if she sent you this?

> "Sorry I was late for the lunch meeting, you guys. My bad. I overslept on accident cuz I felt really yucky and had to run to the little girls' room all nite. Then my car wouldn't start cuz I let the battery run down. For realz! I hope you guys didn't wait a long time. Anyways, lunch

was really nummy even tho veggies aren't my faves!"

Would I give this person serious consideration for a promotion? Nuh-uh. And if you think I'm being too critical, well... you're not the boss of me!

Hypnotism by PowerPoint

Have you ever seen one of those stage hypnotists who grabs people from the audience and, in less than a minute, has them clucking like chickens or doing other ridiculous things? I had always suspected the audience members of being shills, part of the act. But after a couple of decades working for very large companies, I'm beginning to believe such hypnotism is possible. And I think PowerPoint is in on it.

Imagine you're in a warm, darkened conference room. It's just after lunch and you had the two-enchilada special with an ice cream sundae for dessert. Sun is shining, surf's up, and you'd rather be anywhere but in this dreary meeting. The presenter drones on and on about some statistics that don't concern you, and you struggle to look interested. Then it happens.

The presenter laughs sheepishly and apologizes for what's called—in big business—an eye chart. It's a slide so busy and unreadable that no one expects you to digest what's on it. This one is an actual example, and the company name has been hidden to protect the guilty. The colors range from bright chartreuse to a retina-damaging fuchsia.

I could not make this up:

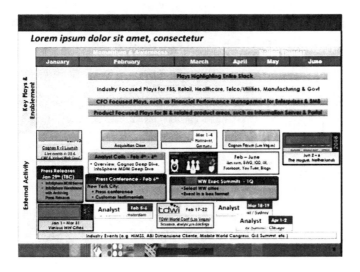

In violating nearly every rule for effective presentation slides, it displays:

1. Too much information

2. Small, unreadable lettering

3. Confusion of shapes

4. Kaleidoscope of colors

5. No single discernible message

At this point, the audience has slipped into a stupor, clearly an altered state. Although I've never seen it happen, I expect them all to start imitating barnyard animals at any moment.

The lesson is this: Keep your PowerPoint slides simple, use bulleted lists with few words and no more than seven bullets. Stick to a harmonious color scheme and make sure the illustrations support the message instead of distracting from it. Use lettering that's large enough to read easily.

Unless your boss is in the room and you want to try a post-hypnotic suggestion... *When I count to three, you will wake up and give me a raise...*

Who Are These
—————————— Jersey Boys?

I witnessed a painful—yet funny—violation of communication's number one commandment (Know Thy Audience) several years ago. The company I worked for in Southern California had been acquired by a mega-huge company based in New York. Our small local enclave included a few hundred people, mostly young software engineers, many from other countries.

Here's the scene: Southern Cal, many developer types, lots of people who grew up in other cultures. A mere handful of people old enough to remember the sixties. An important executive came from the mother ship in New York to address us in an outdoor garden meeting.

The company had paid his airfare, hotel, meals, and ground transportation. He had a thirty-minute speech planned and, by George, he was going to deliver every word of it no matter what. He began by asking enthusiastically, "Show of hands—who has seen *Jersey Boys*?" Not a single hand went up.

First, it's California. Years before the *Jersey Boys* movie came out. A traveling company of the Broadway hit show had played the West Coast, but it was in San Diego, and it had closed more than a year before. Second, San Diego theater events are not well publicized in Orange County. Third, your average group of software developers is not typically a musical theater crowd.

But, undeterred, our speaker went on for twenty-nine more minutes metaphorically describing our corporate future in terms of some deep philosophical truths illustrated by the struggles of Frankie Valli and the Four Seasons. It appeared that no one in the audience had a clue what he was talking about. At least he didn't sing.

When you write or speak in a business context, or any other for that matter, your first consideration should be a good audience definition. Think about these audience characteristics:

- Age

- Culture

- Gender

- Interests

- Education level

- Technical sophistication

Ask yourself:

- What characteristics do they have in common?

- What do they care about?

- What resonates with them?

- What is most likely to capture their interest?

Do some homework, ask questions, try to find out as much as you can before writing or speaking to a group. Everyone has seen film clips of jet-lagged, hung-over rock musicians shouting, "Hello Detroit!" when they were actually in Chicago. Nothing falls flatter than a presentation clearly meant for someone else.

The next time you compose a letter, announcement, email, presentation, or speech, try to imagine the confusion I saw on the face of a young engineer from India, leaving the garden meeting where he had sat patiently for more than thirty minutes. As the crowd filed back to their desks, he asked a colleague, "Who are these Jersey Boys?"

His friend shrugged, "Damned if I know."

Your Mission, Should You Choose to Accept It

Anyone who starts a new company seems to go through this process: "We have an office, a website, and a stapler. Good. Now we need a mission statement." Companies agonize over mission statements.

I've seen committees struggle with the task for weeks and still produce nothing. They want a mission statement to sound grandiose without actually promising anything they can be forced to deliver on later. It's a delicate balance.

Business clichés to the rescue! These overworked expressions have reached the status of dialect in many large companies— or small companies trying to act like large ones. A kind of nerdy patois masquerading as cool and confident. The bad news is that these clichés mean almost nothing. The good news is that they mean almost nothing. There's very little to be accountable for if you fail to deliver on your lofty promises.

Sure, the language might be trendy, and it will be so-five-minutes-ago in a couple of years, but let's face it. If you're having this much trouble composing a mission statement, what are the chances you'll still be in business by the time your language is dated?

So I'm going to make it easy. Here's a kind of Mad-Libs for mission statements you can use to write your own. Place any word or expression from a numbered group into the corresponding numbered slot in the Instant Mission Statement.

- **Group 1**—ROIs, paradigms, best practices, ecosystems, solutions, corporate values, core competencies, learnings, opportunities

- **Group 2**—scalable, best-of-breed, bleeding edge, state of the art, cost-effective, amazing, robust, user-friendly, impactful

- **Group 3**—leverage, utilize, incentivize, optimize, consumerize, analyze, synergize, monetize, productize

- **Group 4**—think outside the box, take it to the next level, eat our own dog food, blow away the competition, take a 30,000-foot view, close the loop, pick the low-hanging fruit, get our ducks in a row, give 110%

- **Group 5**—phone it in, boil the ocean, throw in the towel, flake out, cave in, miss the boat, hit the skids, go belly up, call it quits

Instant Mission Statement

Our company is built on solid principles and time-tested traditions with the highest professionalism and integrity. Our mission is to deliver satisfaction through the finest -1- available. Our offerings are always -2- and we -3- our results better than anyone else. Even in difficult times, we will always -4- and we will never -5-. This is our mission, our goal, our promise, and at the end of the day—it is what it is.

Voila! A mission statement in two minutes. Try it—it's easy. Who knows? You might even decide to start a company.

I think that'd be, like, awesome.

——————— World Renounced Doctor

In a medical office waiting room, I noticed one of those flat-screen monitors with messages about health issues, interspersed with promos for various doctors affiliated with the practice.

The idea is to give you something besides old magazines to read and to remind you to eat healthful food and get lots of exercise... while you're waiting to see the doctor who's going to tell you to eat healthful food and get more exercise.

One of the promos caught my eye because it said a doctor in the practice was a *world renounced surgeon*. It went on to list his many accomplishments. Obviously, they meant *renowned* (eminent, distinguished, and famous). I knew the front desk staff was not responsible for the message content, but I thought they might tell someone who was. When I mentioned the error to them, they gave me a blank stare.

I tried to explain that *renounced* means disclaimed, disavowed, abandoned, and that I didn't think they wanted to be saying that about the good doctor. More blank stares. Finally, one of them chirped, "Oh—I guess that's the other meaning."

By now I'm yelling to myself inside my head. No, it's two different words! There is no other meaning! The receptionist gave me a patronizing smile and went back to her paperwork. So I went back to reading old magazines.

I've often seen *renowned* misspelled as *reknown* or *reknowned,* I suppose because there is a vague sense that it means well-known, and it seems logical to put a letter k in it. But I'd never seen it confused in such a public way with a word that means almost the opposite.

The experience made me question whether, in trying to do the doctor a favor, I had overstepped. I was polite, but the staff reacted as if I were speaking a foreign language or had wandered out of the ward without my meds.

I started to think… if the word was intentional, that raises several disturbing possibilities. I guess it depends on who has renounced him and what they renounced him for. It must have been pretty big because it did say *world renounced.*

- If he's a surgeon by day and a superhero by night, and he has been renounced by the Forces of Evil, I admire him.

- If the AMA or the state medical licensing board has renounced him, he might be practicing medicine illegally.

- If his wife has left him and is posting it to Facebook friends all over the globe, it's unfortunate but it's really none of my business.

Maybe the message should have been more specific.

—————————— Credit Card Crimes

You'd think huge companies with billions in assets could afford good writers and editors to create their customer notification letters. But credit card companies and banks are among the worst communicators of all. Although I'm all for fighting crime, credit card fraud is not the only crime involved in this story.

My credit card statement recently showed two in-store purchases for twelve hundred dollars at a home improvement store in New York. But I hadn't been within two thousand miles of New York for more than a year. I called the bank, and a fraud investigation followed. The bank cancelled the card and sent me a new one.

To follow up, their fraud department sent me a paper form to check and sign, just to verify our phone conversations. Although I appreciated their swift resolution of the fraud issue, I was surprised at the poorly written checklist. Here is one example:

____ The credit card was in my and anyone authorized to use my account's possession on the date that the fraudulent transactions occurred.

Authorized to use my account's possession? The long phrase sandwiched between the first *my* and *possession* gums up the meaning of the sentence and compels the reader to re-read it. It's a case of What Happens when you try to stuff parenthetical information between words that should stay together. I understand they're trying to cover two situations in one sentence, but it doesn't work. Here's one way they might have handled it:

On the date of the fraudulent transactions, the credit card was not in:

_____ my possession.

_____ the possession of anyone authorized to use my account.

Another instruction said:

Please draw a line through any transactions that were authorized by you in black ink.

Authorized by me in black ink? I authorized nothing in any kind of ink. No ink. That's the idea of a <bleeping> credit card. How about:

> Using black ink, draw a line through
> any transactions you authorized.

Better yet, the company could move into the current century and spring for an imaging system that reads other ink colors. Say, blue.

Huge companies have millions of customers, many of whom are poor readers. Others are busy and impatient, or they struggle with English. A tiny investment in clear communication might prevent revenue losses—the results of misunderstanding—extra phone calls, and customer churn.

Perhaps I should have responded, on a separate sheet of paper:

> The depth of my and anyone authorized to use my account's bewilderment at the well intentioned I'm sure directions on this form your Customer Service or Fraud Units probably in good faith composed make it impossible that I and anyone authorized to use my account's understanding of how to accurately and completely respond to the questions in black ink would enable us to use this account.
>
> I and anyone authorized to use my account are, herewith, cutting up our credit cards and burying our cash in a coffee can in the back yard.

Faking Friendly

P olite expressions are like condiments. Just the right amount of mustard on a sandwich is delicious, but you wouldn't eat an entire jar of it with a spoon as if it were yogurt.

Customer Service Representatives (CSRs) have my deepest sympathy. It's tough to remain sane when you deal with angry people all day. Many companies train their CSRs in techniques to defuse complaints and calm unreasonable callers. But along the way, some have gone overboard with fawning pretend-friendliness.

Anyone who calls Customer Service in search of a new best friend needs to get a hobby. It's as if someone decided that, if a little politeness is good, a truckload of bowing and scraping is that much better. But there is a point where it becomes more annoying than helpful. Here's a recent conversation I had with my bank's CSR:

Your name, please? [answer]

Fantastic! Thank you sooooo much! How are you today? [Fine]

That's just woooooonderful! Last four digits of your Social? [answer]

Thank you soooooooo very much! How are you doing today? [Mmm... fine.]

Oooooooh! Outstanding! Security code? [answer]

Greeeeeaaaaat! Thank you so very much! So how's your day going? [Uh... fine.]

That's just awesome! How can I help you? [answer... resolution]

Thank you so very much for calling. We soooooooo appreciate your business and you have just a super-fantastic day!

The falling-down-grateful act seemed a bit much for simply giving my account information. I didn't donate a kidney. The obsession with my day was cloying and excessive, especially since (1) the person doesn't know me or care about my day, (2) it's none of anyone's business, and (3) I just said it was fine. Three times.

What can we learn from this? It seems counter-intuitive, but in business communication you don't need to preface every direction with *Please*. Please feel free to contact us. Please see enclosed coupon. Please press the Enter key. It's not even necessary to say "Thank you" at the end of a presentation. Simply conclude and invite questions. Fake courtesy feels disingenuous and, in some cultures, weak or condescending. Pleasant, professional responses and problem-solving are more effective—in person, on the phone, and in writing.

I'm toying with a canned answer to the oft-repeated "How is your day going?" question for the next time I'm asked. I would say it in that rapid-fire speech they use for disclaimers in radio commercials. It would sound something like this:

> "Oh I'm so glad you asked because no one around here really cares how my day is going you know for thirty years my arthritis has been acting up and with the change in weather all my joints hurt my doctor says there's nothing he can do but I don't trust him not that my kids would care or call or come and visit goodness knows I was always there to take care of them when they needed anything but take care of Mom nosiree Bob maybe if this rain clears up my joints won't ache and I'll be able to call up Marge and go to bingo..."

I wonder if they would ask me a second time.

————————————————— Audio Clutter

I like Norah Jones. Norah Jones makes pleasant music that goes well with relaxing in a social setting, and I enjoy listening to it. Unless I'm trying to hear Customer Service instructions over it, and they are playing at about equal volumes. I recently called a company and got their phone tree of selections. It sounded like this:

> My heart is drenched in wine But you'll be on my mind Forever Out across the endless sea I would die in ecstasy But I'll be a bag of bones Driving down the road alone My heart is drenched in wine But you'll be on
> my mind Forever Something has to make
> **Hello. Thank you for calling [Business** you run I don't know why I didn't come I
> feel as **name]. If you wish to speak to a** why I
> **Customer Service Representative, please**
> I don't know why I didn't come I waited 'til I
> saw the sun I do **press three.** why I didn't come
> I left you by the house of fun I don't know why I didn't come I don't know why I didn't come When I saw the break of day I wished that I could fly away Instead of kneeling in the sand Catching teardrops in my hand

The audio clutter was so bad I could hardly hear the business message. Imagine trying to decipher it with a bad cell phone connection. As I waited on hold, the Norah Jones song ended and Barry White took over. And it wasn't just hold music. It continued throughout the entire conversation, even after the representative came on the line. Not softly in the background, but loud. The rep was a young woman with a small voice and a heavy accent, and as I struggled to understand her, this is what I heard:

I've heard people say that too much of anything is not good for you, baby, but I don't know about that As many times as we've loved, and We've shared love, and

Hello. This is June. How may I help you today? OK, I see. You would like to correct the name of the recipient? What is your order number, please? Just a moment please ...

enough, of your love, baby, Girl, I don't know, I don't know why I can't get enough of your love babe Some things I can't get used to, no matter I try It's like the more you give, the more I want And baby, that's no lie, oh no, baby Tell me, what can I say, what am I gonna do? How should I

During her speech, Barry did that thing where he talks through an interlude instead of singing. So he's pouring out his heartfelt declarations of love in that luscious caramel-syrup voice, and she wants my order number. It was as if they were battling for my attention. She put me on hold for several minutes, during which Barry finished the song and it was back to Norah Jones. Only two songs on the audio loop, and they never stopped. Barry's message was pretty clear (Ooooh baby, baby, know what I'm sayin' girl?), but I'm not so sure about the Customer Service rep's.

If you do business on the phone, make sure the conversations you have with customers are clear and understandable. Here are some guidelines:

1. A lot of music is wildly inappropriate for a business setting.

2. Hold music, if you must have it, should be instrumental, not vocal.

3. Hold music, if you must have it, stops when a voice, live or recorded, is on the line.

4. A Customer Service representative should be able to speak in a clear voice, with good pronunciation, and without background noise. That includes noise from other representatives on other calls.

Music is subjective. One person's favorite is another's greatest annoyance. Years ago, I worked for a manufacturing company that decided we would all be more productive if we were forced to listen to piped-in music from a local radio station. All day long. Throughout the building. On the production floor, in every office, in the parking lot, and on the phones. Even in the restrooms. We were treated like contented cows in a barn. Some of the less-contented cows hated it so much they climbed up on their desks in their high-heeled shoes and disconnected the ceiling speaker wires. Or so I've heard—not that I would ever do such a thing.

Management refused to acknowledge employee complaints until the day they discovered that the radio station ran frequent ads for a competitor. So when phone customers were put on hold, they were listening to commercials for a competitor's products, which—we all had to admit—were better than ours.

I'm sure the music wasn't completely to blame, but the Einsteins running this company were astonished when it finally went out of business... go figure.

Four Steps to
————————— Marketing Speak

D id you ever read product information on a web site and wonder what the <bleep> they're selling? An Emperor's New Clothes mystique surrounds much of today's business marketing copy. The reader has no idea what it means, but is afraid to admit it. The writers think they've impressed their audience and everyone pretends the words mean something.

It seems hard, but you too can learn to write like this. Here are four tips to help you write turgid, meaningless copy that will confuse everyone... especially your customers.

1. Pile on the buzzwords

> No marketing text is complete without at least five of these faddish obfuscators (like that one?):
>
> Leverage, impact (as a verb), solutions, processes, issues, utilize, maximize, minimize, digitize, systematize, productize, strategize,

optimize, dramatically, functionality, capabilities, efficiencies.

2. Loooooong sentences

String together as many subordinate clauses, parenthetical expressions, noun clumps, and gerunds as possible.

3. Modifiers

Bring on the adjectives, adverbs, and entire phrases to describe whatever you're selling, but don't reveal what it actually is.

4. Prepositional phrases

Nothing puffs up your description like lots of prepositions.

Here is a before-and-after illustration that shows how you can take a clear idea and translate it into Marketing-speak.

Example—before

Our software products handle invoices, accounts, and service requests. They do it better than the manual way you're probably doing it now. Save money, serve your customers promptly, stand out from your competitors, and see your business increase. Call us today.

Example—after

> Organizations like yours leveraging manual, resource-intensive, complex, and error-prone processes can significantly increase their responsiveness to customers in information-intensive, real-time interactions, dramatically maximize their level of service, gain competitive advantage over others, and better manage and grow their businesses while also greatly reducing operating costs by utilizing the functionality and capabilities of our solutions.

Satire alert—Do not try this at home.

No, really. Don't.

What's in a Name?

Sometimes the names we're born with don't go well with businesses or jobs we choose as adults. You can change your name, of course, or just put up with the jokes if the name sounds funny with your chosen occupation.

But if you're naming a business, it's wise to give serious thought to your choice.

I've heard of several orthopedic surgeons and dentists name Dr. Payne. Those professions would also be problematic if your name were Hertz. Try saying to your six-year-old, "Get your jacket, we're going to see Dr. Hertz." Picture struggling to stuff Garfield into a cat carrier when he knows he's going to the vet.

There are a few dentists named Dr. Chu, but that one's just cute.

Dr. Dement, a professor of psychiatry at Stanford, must have a sense of humor. The former Archbishop of Manila, Jaime Sin, enjoyed a good laugh when people called him Cardinal Sin."

Whalen is an unfortunate name to have if you're an animal rights activist. Griese is not a good name for a gourmet chef, a lawyer named Cheatham is a walking punchline, and—I couldn't make this up—there is actually a Dye Funeral Home. If you've grown up with a strange name all your life, it has lost its strangeness and just sounds like family to you. You might be proud of it, but if your fine old family name is Hitler or Bin Laden, please call your business something else.

On a Virginia highway, I once saw a panel truck with this sign: *Peed Plumbing—let your drains flow freely.* I hope that's a family name, because if someone chose it for the business, that's just so wrong.

If your business might relocate, don't name it after the original location. Blackstone TV and Appliance moved from Blackstone Avenue to Cedar Avenue, but it's still named Blackstone TV and Appliance. Shields Medical Clinic long ago moved from Shields Avenue to Herndon Avenue, but it's still called Shields Medical Clinic. Even if you think you're never moving, no one knows what the future holds. You can't easily rename your business just because you lost your lease.

At least think about how your business name looks on a sign or a truck, and be careful about spacing and placement of the words. Yesterday I saw a big, heavy truck with this sign on the door:

AAA Battery

Delivery & Installation

Aren't AAA batteries those tiny ones that power small electronic devices? You need a truck to deliver those?

When You Open
—————————Your Mouth

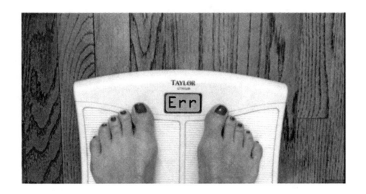

ave you ever admired someone's writing, only to be
shocked when you saw them interviewed on television?
Or listened to an audio clip of the author reading her
own book? Even intelligent and erudite people (in print) can
spoil the illusion with careless pronunciation or annoying
vocal habits. It reminds me of stories about the first movies
that came out with sound, when the stars of the silent screen
were heard for the first time. Suddenly the leading man with
the smoldering eyes didn't seem so romantic when you heard
his squeaky voice. More than one silent film star saw the end
of his career when talkies became the standard.

Pronunciation, tone of voice, even the subtle undertones that
betray feelings you're trying to hide… all of these factors can
undermine the effectiveness of your vocal communication.

This holds true whether you're in a one-on-one sales situation or you're addressing a packed auditorium at a business conference.

If you have a good message, you don't have to be formally trained to be a successful speaker. You just have to be aware of how you sound to others and avoid the habits that could torpedo your communication. Record your voice and listen to yourself. If you sound like a cartoon character or a reality show "star," consider communicating in writing.

Vocalized Pauses

It all started when I stepped on my digital bathroom scale and the display said Err instead of a number. My first thought was that it was stalling, trying to find the words to deliver some bad news.

I thought of my high school speech teacher who introduced me to the term *vocalized pauses*. Those fillers that come out of our mouths while we're waiting for the brain to engage and provide actual words. Usually when the situation is stressful or awkward. It's as if we think "Err, mmmm, aaah, well, you see, uuuh…" is better than nothing.

I realize my scale was just telling me that it needs a new battery, but I took it personally. For an instant I was back in high school, with the cool kids yelling, "Hey Olive Oyl! Skinny Minnie!" Or worse, singing "Bony Maronie–she's as skinny as a stick of macaroni!" Thank you, Larry Williams, for that rock and roll gem–the soundtrack to my adolescence.

When you're speaking to a group, whether it's a small meeting or an auditorium full of people, do whatever you can to avoid vocalized pauses. The best solution is to be well prepared and know your material thoroughly. But if you feel a vocalized pause coming on, do one of these:

Swallow.

Gesture.

Take a breath.

Sip some water.

Bite your tongue.

Pretend the silence is for dramatic effect

Vocalized pauses communicate a lack of confidence and cast suspicion on your message. It's as if you're hedging, trying to think of a way to say something unpleasant or even untruthful.

The scale experience did give me an idea, though. If someone has not already invented this, someone needs to. A programmable scale that delivers messages as your weight approaches a target number, up or down.

My Fitbit sends me encouragement when I'm close to my daily target walking distance. Just five hundred more steps! If I reach or exceed my daily goal, I get little badges and congratulatory messages. Since January 1, you have walked the length of California!

A bathroom scale should do that. You set the target weight and gender. Whether you're too thin (and trying to gain a little) or too heavy (and trying to lose), the display could say:

> Don't worry—it takes time!

> You'll get there—don't give up!

> Keep at it—just fifteen more pounds!

> Five more pounds—you're awesome!

> Lookin' good, girl!

The deluxe model might offer recorded messages voiced by— say—George Clooney or the celebrity of your choice.

It sounds silly, but who wants a bathroom scale that can't find the words to tell you the truth? It's as bad as listening to a speech full of, "You know? Uh, mmm, like, well..."

Anything is better than that.

Yeh-yeh-yeh, Perfect!

I recently went to lunch with two friends. The restaurant was not crowded, and I told the young hostess, "We'd like a table for thr—" but before I could finish, she interrupted, "Yeh-yeh-yeh, follow me."

This expression, a carryover from social conversation, might work when several people are talking at once and everyone is in a hurry. But it pops up far too often in conversation that doesn't warrant it.

The hostess smiled and was pleasant. But the implication was still "Get to the point already. Stop talking. OK, now you're boring me." After I'd spoken only five words, that hardly seemed fair.

Faddish social conversation creeps into business usage as people devalue words that should be reserved for something special. A routine call to a hair salon sounds like this:

I'd like an appointment. "Awesome!"

How about Thursday? "Fantastic!"

Could I have three o'clock? "Fabulous!"

OK, it's on my calendar. "Perrrrrfeeeect!"

All I did was schedule a haircut and I'm bleeping amazing, phenomenal, and leave no room for improvement. Really (blushing), it was nothing...

A young retail clerk told me the shop was having a fifty percent off sale. She gushed, "We've sold literally millions of these jeans. It's amaz!" Literally? Millions? I doubt that. I guess she was too exhausted from selling all those jeans to finish pronouncing the word *amazing*.

Young people have a social language that works for them. I get that. In a creative business or a twenty-somethings hangout, social language is just fine. But if your career target is dealing with the general public or corporate America, many people won't appreciate or understand it.

Those devalued superlative words find their way into emails, newsletters, and sales presentations. Older readers just see it as exaggeration and discount it. Lack of communication awareness in business can be a barrier to advancement in many jobs. Instead of conveying energy and cool factor, it suggests immaturity and poor judgment.

Maybe it should be a rite of passage, at a certain age, to re-examine communication habits for business. If you're still writing and speaking at work the way you talked at school or when you're out with friends, it might be time to recalibrate.

Remember that trendy is temporary. In 1996, for about twenty minutes, the hottest thing going was the Macarena (look it up). And everyone was saying yada-yada-yada (Seinfeld reference).

You whippersnappers with your Facebooks and tweets and newfangled nonsense—learn to communicate with grownups for crying out loud. Why, back in my day... proper English was taught in school... youngsters respected their elders... yeh-yeh-yeh. OK, now I'm boring myself.

—————————————— Uptalk? Anyone?

A few years ago a peculiar speech affectation was popular among adolescent girls. Today, this quirk has spread beyond the teenybopper set and crept into the speech of men as well as women, and even into business and technical communities. Maybe the teenyboppers just grew up, or at least got older.

It's called Uptalk. With Uptalk, the tone of voice in every sentence rises at the end, as if it were a question.

> So I'm, like, no way?

> And she goes, yes way?

> And I'm all, OMG?

> And she's, like, seriously?

> … and so on.

Listen closely the next time you hear a—probably young—person give a webinar or explain how to do something technical.

So here's our Technical Director, George? He's going to tell us about the new features in our latest release? We have some great new upgrades you're going to like? Many of these ideas came from our customers?

The trouble with Uptalk is that it makes everything you say sound weak and tentative. The invisible question mark in your voice implies "I'm sorry—I think—I'm not sure—I mean—is that all right with you?" If you're trying to be authoritative, the habit undermines everything you say.

Akin to Uptalk, another speech anomaly is threatening to infect our communications. You might recognize it as a groaning elongation of the last syllable in every sentence. It works best if you really give the long syllable a good, guttural quality that says "I'm so bored I can hardly get this word ooooouuuut." It is prevalent on a TV show in which everyone tries to keep up with a family whose names all begin with K.

That's the best bikini ev-eeeer?

Let's have lunch—I'm hungr-yyyy?

Those shoes are so raaaad?

Turns out this phenomenon has a name too: vocal fry. I've been calling it K-groan, for lack of a better description. It always seems to accompany Uptalk. When you combine these effects, you create the perfect storm of bad communication. It implies "I'm not sure about this, but I'm so bored to be talking to you that I really don't care."

I listened to an audiobook sample the other day in which the author, an authority on grammar, had done her own voice-over. I decided to pass when she groaned, "I've been doing this for fifteen yeeeeaaaars?" The tone was exactly as if she had just stepped out of that TV reality show. It blew her credibility right there.

Uptalk, vocal fry, or K-groan, leave the speech distortions to those who don't care about their credibility. Ya knoooow? Like, reallyyyy? It's so stupiiiid? I'm seriouuuus?

—————————Has it All Been Said?

Social media channels are touted as useful tools for net-working and sharing ideas. Some are full of inane chatter and photos of what you ate for breakfast, but a few people have found a way to make it even more absurd, if that's possible. They spend all day posting nothing but links to articles other people have written.

A good online discussion needs original thoughts. People disagree, they have different viewpoints. They make good arguments or they don't. They sometimes support each other and find common ground. It takes a little effort and imagination. The interaction is what makes it interesting.

Maybe there is nothing new to be said. Maybe these compulsive link-senders don't realize that if we wanted links, we would subscribe to newsfeeds. I see one Tweeter who posts about a hundred fifty links per day, some of them multiple times. In the time she took to do that, she might have written something interesting and original.

I've noticed the same trend in LinkedIn discussion groups. Instead of initiating topics and exchanging ideas, participants are just posting articles from the Wall Street Journal or Harvard Business Review. Often there is no thread of common interest, no discussion.

We all share links with individuals when we know the recipient is interested in the subject. But using Twitter or discussion groups to blast people indiscriminately is just spam by any other name.

It reminds me of people I knew, before the days of social media, who loved to memorize quotations. Rather than expressing their own thoughts, they responded in conversation like this:

> What do you think about that?
>
> > Well, Abraham Lincoln once said…
>
> Yes, but what do you think?
>
> > As Lyndon Johnson stated in his inaugural address…
>
> OK, but what do you…
>
> > I believe Winston Churchill put it best when he…
>
> Do you have an opinion?
>
> > In the words of Christopher Marlowe…
>
> [Sound of footsteps as I walk away…]

If the quote is right on target, it's one thing. But most of the time it's only marginally applicable and the recitation is just a performance opportunity. Look at me! I memorized something. Look at me! I found an article. Look at me! I have nothing to say so I'm recycling someone else's words.

It's like a Kafka-esque dream. A slick salesman rings your doorbell. Every time you open the door, he launches into a canned speech about a different product. He won't go away. He keeps ringing the bell. Each time a different canned speech, a different product. He stands there all day and never tires of the routine. Your choices are to ignore the doorbell or disconnect it.

It's enough to make you long for a cute, awkward child selling Girl Scout cookies.

Just Name the Place

If you want to pick a fight with people, all you have to do is mispronounce the names of their hometowns. The United States, more like a patchwork quilt than a melting pot at times, is a great place to start.

Our city names with roots in Native American, Spanish, French, and other languages provide endless fodder for heated debate. Some pronunciations have remained true to their origins, while others have morphed into something unrecognizable. A few names borrowed from other cultures seem deliberately twisted as if to apply a local stamp of ownership.

To be fair, Americans themselves mispronounce city names all the time. But we grow righteously indignant when someone from England, Australia, Canada, or Mexico does it.

The American Southwest has countless cities with Spanish names. The number of city names beginning with *Las*, *Los*, *San*, or *Santa* alone is staggering. Some are pronounced the same way by people both north and south of the Rio Grande. For instance, San Jose is just *san ho-SAY*. Los Angeles, however, is another matter. If you're a local you probably pronounce it something like *lahss AN ja less*, not *loce AHN heh lace*, unless you also speak Spanish.

But pity the poor tourist who says *loss AN ja leez*. It's not the plural of a Greek-origin word like *crisis* for crying out loud. One crisis, two crises. One Los Angelis, two Los Angeleez? Jeez!

There's a Newark in New Jersey that's pronounced *NOO-erk*. But there's also a Newark in Delaware that's pronounced *noo ARK*. That's right—as in—Noah replacing his boat.

Las Vegas (no, not *Lost Wages*) is from Spanish. So the first syllable rhymes with *mas*, not *mass*.

People from Spokane, Washington, a city with Native American roots, bristle when others pronounce it *spo CANE* instead of *spo CAN*.

In the Big Easy, they don't like you to say *noo OR lee uns* in four syllables. Most tourists get by with a middle-of-the-road *noo OR lins* although the natives just shorten it to *nawlns*, which rolls around inside the mouth and falls out in one under-articulated syllable.

A town in Indiana named Versailles is pronounced—I'm not making this up—*vur SALES*. I don't recommend using that pronunciation if you're visiting the palace and gardens in France. But if you're in Indiana and call it *vare SIGH*, you'll be instantly tagged as a troublemaker and the sheriff will probably follow you around until you leave.

I understand Aussies get annoyed when people pronounce Melbourne *MELL burn* instead of *MELL bin*. And the British can be generally impatient with all American pronunciations. But, really, what can you expect when you spell something C-H-O-L-O-M-O-N-D-L-E-Y and pronounce it *CHUM lee*? What a waste of perfectly good letters.

In short, travelers would do well to find out the correct local pronunciations of places they visit. It helps you avoid condescending looks, enhances your enjoyment of the trip, and makes you thankful you're not going home to that village in Wales called:

Llanfairpwllgwyngyllgogerychwyrn-
drobwllllantysiliogogogoch.

When tourists are not around, I hear the locals just call it Llanfairpwllgwyngyll for short.

All in the Delivery

In an often-quoted comment, someone once said that America and England are two nations divided by a common language. It's variously attributed to Winston Churchill, George Bernard Shaw, and Oscar Wilde.

Regardless of who said it first, it's true. Even if you are careful about slang terms or those known to be different (lorry-truck, lift-elevator, flat-apartment), accents and pronunciations can interfere with the understanding of even a common spoken language.

The United States, large in area and culturally diverse, has many baffling regional pronunciations. If you're a Texan addressing a large audience, many people will not understand, *Mah daddy's in thuh awl bidness.* If you're from Lowong Guyland Noo Yak, southerners might not get, *Cawl us at foah-foah-foah three-noin-two-foah.* And we all live in the same country.

My favorite story about English misunderstanding is a true, but Monty-Python-worthy, incident. A British-born friend of mine was going through the naturalization process to become a US citizen. He had dutifully gone to the court house, filled out all the required papers, waited all the appropriate times, and jumped through all the appropriate hoops. But a worker at the court house window (obviously an immigrant himself) told him there was one more hoop:

You haff pass engrshlngshtess.

What's that again?

Engrshlngshtess. You haff pass engrshlngshtess.

By this time, I can imagine the light dawning as my friend grasped the irony. He was being told he had to pass an English language test... by someone whose own English was unintelligible.

My friend the Brit was far too polite to say it, but I'm sure he was thinking, "English language test? Are you daft? I'm from ENGLAND! We <bleeping> invented it! Just feast your ears on these beautifully articulated consonants!"

Good story to bear in mind if you're asked to give a presentation to a large audience. Even if your audience consists entirely of native English-speakers (remember that includes Canadians, Aussies, and many others), it's a good idea to:

1. Speak a little more slowly than usual

2. Enunciate clearly

3. Avoid slang and idioms

4. Project your voice, even if you're using a microphone. Don't swallow your words.

5. Use slides with the most important bullet points written on them

6. Invite questions at the end, in case you need to clarify

So give your presentation, even if you don't fancy it, though the beastly thing is all at sixes and sevens and you need another fortnight to prepare. Never mind it feels all fur-coat-and-no-knickers, life's not all beer and skittles. Sticky wicket if it's your job, but don't be cheeky with your boss and risk getting sacked. Stiff upper lip, enunciate, and knock the audience on its collective bum.

Medical Jeopardy

America's population is aging, and all of us will eventually be afflicted with some medical condition or other. No one is expected to spell and pronounce them all correctly, but if it's your ailment, you can at least make an effort.

You probably know some codger who complains about his Arthur Itus (arthritis) or very close veins (varicose veins). And he might have a friend with Al Heimers (Alzheimer's) or pain in his sackarilliac (sacroiliac). He might even have an annerism (aneurism) or a heart attact (heart attack).

But if you're writing or speaking for the public, there is no excuse for some of the errors I've seen recently. Correct spellings and pronunciations are available from countless sources. Mangled medical terms in print make me think of the TV game Jeopardy. Silly answers demand silly questions.

- Lime disease (Lyme disease) [What do you get from drinking too many margaritas?]

- Planter fashionitis (plantar fasciitis) [What is a farmer's obsession with what to wear?]

- Lumber pain (lumbar pain) [What do you feel when you get the bill for that new deck?]

- Gangreen (gangrene) [What do street thugs wear on St. Patrick's Day?]

If you want sympathy for your medical condition, try to avoid getting Creutzfeldt-Jakob disease or Mandibulofacial Dyostosis. They are impossible to pronounce. And writing their names would fill up your Twitter character allotment before you could even whine about it. If you receive such a diagnosis, ask for a second opinion—something with a shorter name.

May you live a long and healthy life with none of these maladies. But if you do contract something and insist on writing about it, I recommend a disease that's easy to spell and pronounce. Like gout.

Words Aren't Pompous—
People Are

With few exceptions, pompous words have appropriate times, places, and audiences. It's their inappropriate use that makes them offensive. I remain unconvinced that *utilize* needs to exist, but we'll skip that one for now.

Writers on the Frasier TV comedy must have had great fun creating dialog for their condescending, self-important characters. It gave them a chance to use words like *propinquity, soupçon,* and *insouciance.* Most viewers didn't know what they meant, and that was exactly the point.

If we encounter pretentious prose in written form, we can always look up the words or stop reading. But a business meeting with an affected speaker is a special kind of torture. After a minute or two, we're all looking at our watches, making grocery lists, hiding our phones under the table, and checking emails. It's clear that the speaker's goal is to impress, not to communicate.

Here are three words often used (or misused) by poor communicators.

- inchoate

Means partial or incomplete. If you're a lawyer addressing other lawyers, use *inchoate* with my blessing. Otherwise, think about your audience. Spare them the temptation to mutter "puh-leeze" under their collective breath and zone out.

- ascertain

Means find out or determine. As in, "How did you ascertain that data?" If your audience is a group of college professors, they won't even blink. A general business audience will know what you mean, but many will roll their eyes as if you'd worn a tuxedo on casual Friday. So just say find out or determine.

- verbiage

My favorite. No one uses this correctly. When you tell the graphic designer you want some verbiage about your product under the logo, you're saying you want some unnecessarily long-winded, verbose language. Instead of verbiage, say text or words. If you do use it correctly, remember that it has three syllables: VUR-bee-ij, not two syllables, like garbage.

When your purpose is to impress, rather than communicate, you invite your audience to subconsciously lie in wait—hoping you will make a mistake. When you do, they attack without mercy. People love to find fault with a know-it-all.

I once attended a lecture by an arrogant but well dressed woman who spent two hours boring the audience with poly-syllabic—um—verbiage. Her presentation was oddly unsuitable for the topic and as the audience grew restless she droned on, oblivious to their lack of interest. When she left the podium and raised her arm to write on the whiteboard, they broke into loud guffaws. There it was, dangling from the sleeve of her new suit. A red price tag with the word SALE.

Mmmmmm. Karma.

——————— Endangered Syllables

Ozone layer, polar ice cap... lions, tigers, and bears. Dwindling natural resources get news coverage and organizations raise money to protect them. But there's a little-known crisis right under our noses and no one is doing a thing about it.

I'm talking about the noble syllable, usually an a or an o, just sitting there in the middle of a word. Trying to do its job. We spell them for the most part, because Spellchecker and Autocorrect warn us if we leave them out. Unfortunately, those devices don't work on speech.

Children grow up watching television, so they hear statements like this one:

> I'm your Channel Two *meterologist*. This storm
> is *deteriating*, so maybe in a few days we'll have
> *comftorble tempachers*.

How is a child supposed to know it should be:

meteorologist (mee-tee-or-OL-o-gist) six syllables

deteriorating (dee-TEER-ee-or-ate-ing) six syllables

comfortable (COME-for-tah-bul) four syllables

temperatures (TEM-pur-a-choors) four syllables

TV weather people could at least learn the words of their trade. There aren't that many to know. You can forgive hockey announcers for getting a few Russian, French, and Eastern European names wrong, but—really—weather? Even hockey announcers don't leave syllables out of their words... *skate, ice, hat, trick, puck, goal, stick, fight.* OK, those are all one-syllable words, but you get my point.

I know you're asking, "What can I do to help?"

First of all, you can be vigilant about innocent, abused, and forgotten syllables that deserve to be pronounced. Second, you can avoid wasting syllables in words where they don't belong. Such as *athalete, realator,* and *mischievious.*

Once uttered, extra syllables cannot be recycled and inserted into words that need them. They just die a slow and senseless death, littering the verbal landscape with their carcasses. So be a conscientious custodian of the syllables you have. If we waste those entrusted to our care, future generations will not even remember when syllables roamed wild and free. Our descendants will be forced to communicate with cryptic nonsense.

I just hope it's not too late.

Asbestos I Can

This one has always mystified me. I can't figure out why anyone would say it. Today, again, in an otherwise decently written article, there it was. The writer said:

As best as I can tell...

The next time you're tempted to say *As best as...*, think of *asbestos*—a material formerly used in insulation—that has been linked to lung cancer. Not saying this awkward idiom causes lung cancer, but you never know.

Maybe it sounds close to *As best I can tell...* or *As I can best tell...* both of which make grammatical sense, but sound a little pompous. I expect the next phrase to be something like *my good man*. I guess you could inadvertently write that after binge-watching seven hours of Downton Abbey, but there's really no other excuse.

English adjectives and adverbs have three forms—positive, comparative, and superlative. Here are some examples:

good—better—best

well—better—best

fast—faster—fastest

big—bigger—biggest

The superlative form is the ultimate degree possible. It means there is no comparison. It's the maximum. When you say *as* _____ *as,* you're describing one thing compared with another. That calls for the positive form.

As good as gold

As well as possible

As fast as you can

As big as a house

Try substituting the superlative for any of those. It sounds ridiculous.

As best as gold

As best as possible

As fastest as you can

As biggest as a house

When I hear or read *as best as,* I think of a toddler describing a favorite dessert. I like cookies but ice cream is gooder—it's the mostest bestest of all.

Sure it's the bestest now, but years from now, the toddler will discover other culinary delights. Like crème brûlée.

Some things just can't be compared.

People Who Should
——————Know Better

In the olden days, television and radio newscasters were role models of eloquence and diction. Newspapers employed editors who scrutinized all copy and headlines before they went to press. Books from libraries could be trusted to give you, if not accurate information, at least well edited text.

It's easy to blame the Internet for the decay of written and spoken communication, but the process was already underway when the information highway was first being paved. If anything, the Internet just made it easier to go from here to there. So we now have TV anchors who seem to be hired for their looks, online news articles full of third-grade mistakes, and uninformed opinions masquerading as news.

Trustworthy role models are becoming an endangered species, so we have to be more vigilant than ever. It's rude to poke fun at someone who has not had the benefit of a good education. But these observations are all about people who set themselves up as experts or at least examples to be taken seriously. Broadcasters, newspaper writers, lawyers, instructors.

They'll never know anyway, so feel free to laugh at them all you want. Just don't imitate them.

The Online Tutorial
Drinking Game

First, I'm not advocating drinking games here. They're silly and hazardous to your health. What a juvenile activity—sipping booze every time you hear a certain phrase in a movie or TV show.

Still, I can understand why they exist, aside from being an excuse to drink. A repeated word or phrase can become so distracting it totally eclipses the main event. I remember a college professor who loved the word *particularly*. He liked the sound of it so much he slowly articulated all five syllables, savoring it on his tongue as if it were fine chocolate.

Obviously, drinking was not allowed in the classroom. So during his lectures, we began to record one hash-mark every time he said *particularly*. After class, we compared numbers. I think the record was thirty-two. He was so pleased to see us hanging on his every word and writing in our notebooks that he never realized we had zero idea what he was talking about.

Drinking games exist to make fun of overused words, phrases, or actions that draw attention from the real subject. And that brings me to the subject of online tutorials.

There's nothing wrong with the idea of online tutorials. They show us how to do things, for example with software, that we could never figure out for ourselves. At least not from the icons on the screen or from the unreadable, or non-existent, documentation. And anyone, it seems, can make an online tutorial.

Just be aware that if you create a tutorial with a perky narrator who sounds like Alvin and the Chipmunks, your audience might want to slow things down with a drinking game. And if you want to play a drinking game with someone else's tutorial, I suggest listening for these overused expressions:

- **simply**

  We get it. This is easy. You want us to be confident. "So you simply set up the preferences, and simply create a profile, and simply make a few small adjustments, and simply send it to your mailing list. Now we're going to simply find the solution to the Schrödinger equation for the hydrogen atom in arbitrary electric and magnetic fields."

  Saying *simply* doesn't make it simple.

- **go ahead and**

  As if you think we're poised over our keyboards, afraid to touch them for fear of electrocution. "Go ahead and enter your password, and go ahead and log in, and go ahead and click Next. Now we're going to go ahead and start, and then we'll go ahead and click on the arrow."

This is not bungee jumping off the Tacoma Narrows Bridge.

you guys

"So OK you guys, here's a cool way you guys can make a newsletter. Just insert whatever branding you guys use, with the color scheme of (my favorite) you guys's logo."

I won't even get into the issue of gender references. Just leave off the *guys*.

Disclaimer:

This drinking game will not make the tutorial any clearer. If necessary, the audience can simply just go ahead and run the tutorial again. They still might not understand it, but you guys won't care... and neither will they.

Back-formations

What is a back-formation, you ask? In etymology, back-formation is "the process of creating a new lexeme, usually by removing actual or supposed affixes and resulting in a neologism."

Now that we've cleared that up, let's talk about where they come from and how to use them.

First you take a perfectly good noun, like *burglar*. Since it ends in –ar, it sounds like someone who performs an action. But *burglar* was not formed from an existing verb, although it suggests *to burgle*. It's a silly word, but that verb, created from a noun, is an example of a back-formation. *Burgle* is one of the oldest common back-formations, dating back to the late eighteen hundreds.

Comedians often use back-formations because they sound funny, although many of them have become standard and accepted usage in dictionaries and other references. But you can't just take any word and twist it into another part of speech. If a burglar is one who burgles, is a butler one who buttles? Sometimes it just doesn't work.

A few awkward and irritating back-formations have found their way into business communication. They always feel like speed bumps in the conversation. The speaker is going along, doing just fine, and then—wait—what?

Here are some back-formations and words you might say instead.

- surveil (comes from surveillance) Say survey, observe, or monitor.

- liaise (comes from liaison) Say contact or connect.

- conversate (comes from conversation) Say talk or converse.

- enthuse (comes from enthusiasm) Say excite.

These bumbling, awkward words always make me think of a public official in court, being accused of malfeasance in office. I can hear him announcing, "Your Honor, I swear that I have not *malfeased*, I am not currently *malfeasing*, and I shall not *malfease* in the future."

Clunk! (Law and Order gavel sound)

Guilty! Of back-formation.

────────── Why Do They Say That?

Regional pronunciations are always a good subject for heated discussion. Criticize your accent and you might as well insult your state flag or, worse, your favorite football team.

But some common mispronunciations cross regional boundaries, even creeping into national TV broadcasts and news reports.

I've never figured out why some people leave letters out and other people add them. And others change them into completely different letters. Sports announcers employed for their knowledge of the game are often former sports stars, so I suppose they get a pass on *strenth* and *athalete*.

Law enforcement officers, in interviews, sometimes say things like "According to the affidavid, the realator was an assessory to the crime." As long as they're good at catching bad guys, they can pronounce it any way they like.

But when news anchors with perfect teeth and great hair say, "Our top story—a Klu Klux Klan raid in Westmin-i-ster, followed by breaking news on Sosal Security..." I have to wonder what else qualifies them for the job. Besides the teeth and hair, I mean.

Here are some commonly mispronounced words with their correct pronunciations.

- **Social Security**
  SO-shal Se-CURE-i-tee, not SO-sal Se-CURE-i-tee

- **Westminster**
  WEST-min-ster, not WEST-min-i-ster

- **strength**
  strength, not strenth

- **athlete**
  ATH-leet, not ATH-a-leet

- **realtor**
  REEL-tur, not REEL-a-tur (or RILL-a-tur)

- **accessory**
  ack-SESS-a-ree, not a-SESS-a-ree

- **affadavit**
  aff-a-DAY-vit, not aff-a-DAY-vid

- **Ku Klux Klan**
  koo-klux-klan, not kloo-klux-klan

These are equal opportunity mispronunciations. I've heard them from educators, political leaders, and people from all regions of the country. Each one is an example of laziness—just not paying attention. And the habit of mispronouncing a word often leads to misspelling it when you have to write it down.

I miss Walter Cronkite. He was not pretty by today's standards, but his pronunciation was careful and correct. I wonder what he would think of today's news readers who can't agree on Iraq (eye-RACK, eye-ROCK, ee-ROCK?) and Al Quaeda (al-KAY-da, al-KIE-da, awl-KAY-da?).

If Cronkite were applying for a job today, someone would probably grab him and say, "You've got a great voice, Wally, but the 'stache is so seventies and the glasses have to go... don't worry, we'll get you a shave, porcelain veneers, some blue contacts, and a good hairpiece. Maybe a little Botox around the eyes..."

Me, Myself, and I

When I was in elementary school, and dinosaurs roamed the earth, it was considered bad form to acknowledge yourself in writing. Children were taught to write with disembodied voices, as if denying their own existence.

English teachers told us not to write *I this...* or *I that...* and to use passive verbs to avoid the appearance of too much self-interest. Clear, direct statements were somehow immodest and Hemingway was a radical.

Most of us grew up so uncomfortable writing the personal pronouns *I* and *me* that we are still embarrassed about it. I think some of us have probably even passed it on to our children, like a hereditary disease. Many writers and TV newscasters think the solution is to say *myself*. It's as if *myself* is less direct and somehow more humble. The trouble is, *myself* is a reflexive word and the object of the action must also be its originator. Used improperly, it doesn't make sense.

Consider these examples.

- Send an email to Don and *myself.*

- The committee selected Dave, Mike, and *myself.*

- The President and *myself* are concerned about this.

The first two should be *me.* The first is the object of a preposition and the second is the object of a verb. The third should be *I* because it's the subject of the sentence.

When you use *myself* properly, you describe some action that comes back to you.

- I burned myself on a hot pan. (No one can burn yourself but you.)

- I must remind myself to exercise. (No one can remind yourself but you.)

- I don't feel like myself today. (No one can feel like yourself but you.)

Grammatical correctness is great, but the focus here is on clear communication. The word *myself,* like passive voice, is often used in an awkward attempt to redirect attention away from the writer or speaker. It sounds wimpy, as if you're consciously evading responsibility. Add a few passive verbs and you get weasely pseudo-legal-babble.

> I, myself, think the evidence regarding myself provides plausible deniability that the cookie jar was—allegedly—broken, possibly as a result of its being accidentally dropped on the

kitchen floor by (as for myself, I think it was a neighbor or an intruder) a person or persons unknown or my annoying little brother or myself, or maybe it was the dog.

Don't be afraid to admit you broke the cookie jar and face the consequences with courage. (Cue the inspirational music...) Use *I* and *me* with confidence. And remember that it's not immodest to acknowledge your own voice. So go out there and express your very own *self...* because, grammatically, no one else can.

—————— Sense of Community

I love those small-town or neighborhood weekly newspapers, the kind that are staffed largely by volunteers and local contributors. The news items and chitchat are of interest only to those who live in the area, and perhaps not even to all of them.

But they provide excellent examples we can use to teach our children about writing. How not to communicate clearly in writing, that is.

I won't even discuss letters to the editor, because most of them are soapbox rants and to criticize their grammar would be just too easy. It's amazing to note, however, the amount of rage that's generated by garbage collection schedules, tree-trimming regulations, and people who don't clean up after their pets. The best gems of all are from the police and fire reports.

The most common mistakes are unclear pronoun antecedents and misplaced modifiers. Sometimes the writer has tried to jam too many thoughts into one sentence. As a result, you have to read the sentence over and over again, hoping that by sheer force of will you can compel it to make sense.

Here are some real examples, with street addresses disguised to protect the paranoid. Some are from my community, but others were sent to me by friends around the country. Apparently, this phenomenon is widespread.

- A person was reported slumped in the driver's seat in a van on 222nd Street NE and was blocking the roadway. Upon arrival, the driver was contacted and had just run out of gas.

  Sense—If the driver was just arriving and was contacted, who is the person slumped in the driver's seat?

- 1300 block of Shady Lane. 9:20 p.m. A woman reported an unsolicited proposition from a man, who had observed her in her home washing dishes while naked.

  Sense—OK, did they know each other? Did he do the observing from inside or outside her house? And who was naked here? The dishwasher or the observer? Not that it makes a lot of difference, but still…

- 2:28 pm. A purse was stolen from the beach.

  Sense—How do they know it didn't belong to a person? Did the beach report it? Was it full of sand dollars? (sorry)

And, in just seven words, this reported incident manages to generate an unusual number of questions. Clearly a case where more information would have helped. It occurred in the 1400 block of Sailboat Road at 11 a.m. and simply said:

- A bat is stuck to the ceiling.

> **Sense**—Holy animal control, Batman! Is it a sonar-equipped chiropteran mired in flypaper? Dracula caught by the sunrise, afraid to move? Is it even an animal we're talking about? A Louisville Slugger with too much pine tar on it? How did it get up there? Is it still there? Where can I go to find out what happened?

Match that for drama, New York Times.

The next time one of those little community papers lands on your doorstep, don't just toss it into the recycling bin. Sit down and read what's going on in your neighborhood. It will probably be informative, thought-provoking, or even entertaining.

But if it starts making sense, you might have a problem.

——————— With a Defense Like This

Who needs a prosecutor?

I'm all for brevity and efficiency in writing. Confusion often results when you try to cram too much information into one sentence. But journalists, especially headline writers, sometimes go too far.

In ancient times, newspapers, actually printed on paper, forced writers to fit limited spaces. Column inches were like expensive real estate that might be sold to advertisers. Paper-based journalism is still around, but shrinking, and its Internet cousin imposes space limitations of its own. As a result, writers have to pare their text down to bare bones. They start with a clear understanding of what they mean, but important words end up on the cutting room floor. And sometimes those discarded words make all the difference.

Writers misplace modifiers, substitute with short and ambiguous words, and omit critical information. Their articles and headlines provide us with a never-ending stream of funny items we can send to our friends or share in online forums.

Here are some of my favorite blooper headlines.

- Coal Miners Refuse to Work After Death

    The article goes on to explain that a recent fatal mine accident makes workers fear for their lives. The miners believe the mine is unsafe, and will not return to work until the company implements some safety measures. For the sake of three letters, the writer chose *Death* instead of *Accident,* implying that the miners allowed a little thing like being dead to interfere with their duties. I could almost hear certain people saying, "Buncha sissies – that's what you get for letting the unions in!"

- Enraged Cow Injures Farmer with Axe

    Apparently it was the farmer, not a cow with bovine spongiform encephalopathy, who had the axe here. But in the pursuit of brevity someone neglected to clarify that. If it had been the cow—without opposable thumbs—wielding the weapon, that would have been a different story. This version is two letters shorter: Cow Injures Wood-chopping Farmer.

Misleading articles and headlines with misplaced modifiers constitute another category of bloopers in print. Prepositional phrases are often the culprit, but you can't blame them entirely. Poor things, they just do as they're told and don't choose where they're placed.

- Two Sisters Reunited After 18 Years at Checkout Counter

  Turns out the sisters found each other, after an eighteen-year separation, in a chance meeting while shopping. But the headline implies that it took them eighteen years in close proximity (hanging out at a checkout counter?) to realize they were sisters. You'd think one of them might have mentioned Crazy Aunt Ethel, or that foot with six toes, or some other family-specific tidbit. This version has fewer letters: Long Separated, Sisters Reunite at Checkout Counter.

This one isn't a headline, but it has to be my all-time favorite.

- Oklahoma City bomber Timothy McVeigh was cremated and his ashes scattered at an undisclosed location after he was executed by his attorney...

  This writer had no excuse. It was an article, not a tightly spaced headline. In trying to say that the attorney scattered the ashes, he implies legal services also included executing the defendant. One-stop shop. Save the taxpayers some money. No need for a prosecutor, judge, jury, and all that due process nonsense.

  The whole thing could have been avoided by deleting the phrase *after he was executed*. He couldn't have scattered ashes before the defendant was executed, now could he?

I don't know about you, but if I needed a defense attorney, I'd think twice about calling this guy. Just in case.

─────────── Your Honor, I Object!

It's unfair to pick on the uneducated or those who struggle to learn English. But pretenders and pseudo-academics are fair game. A native English-speaking college graduate with a doctorate and a professional title should display a reasonable use of the language. Particularly if that profession requires skillful, sometimes manipulative, use of English... sprinkled with Latin.

Yesterday in a television interview, a prosecuting attorney said in describing a pastor accused of murder:

> This man presented himself to the community
> as a *paradigm* of *virtuosity.*

Where do I begin? One of these would be called a malapropism (a speech error in which a word is nonsensical in context, but similar in sound to the correct word). But two of them in the same sentence! That's difficult to do, even if you're trying.

Let the court transcript show, the correct idiom is:

paragon of virtue

It means a perfect example (paragon) of purity, goodness, or high moral standards (virtue).

Paradigm, a trendy, overused business buzzword, is just a pattern or example. *New paradigm* often refers to a different business model or way of doing things.

And virtuosity means great artistic skill, particularly in music. Jimi Hendrix displayed virtuosity on the electric guitar. Clearly, virtue was not a requirement.

So with this malapropism, the attorney literally accused the pastor of presenting himself to the community as a new way to play a musical instrument. Hardly a crime. But she emphasized that, since he had lied, everything he said was questionable. It follows that, since she spoke nonsense, everything else she said was also questionable.

Errors like these occur when we try to add syllables and make ourselves sound important, assuming the audience won't know the difference. Or when we don't know the difference ourselves.

Ergo, the prosecutor ipso facto displays sufficient mens rea in the actus reus. This posturing, double whammy of grammatical absurdity must be some kind of felony. Don't you hate it when people do that?

Perhaps the defense attorney should have instructed the defendant to stare menacingly at the prosecutor, wearing one of those T-shirts that says "I am silently correcting your grammar."

———————— Sentence Stuffing Quiz

Some things are meant to be stuffed:

- Thanksgiving turkeys

- Antique parlor chairs

- Teddy bears

Some things are not:

- Speedos

- Biking shorts

- Sentences

If you stuff yourself into too-small clothes, the result is both unattractive and uncomfortable. Most people understand this. But when it comes to writing, it's as if there were a prize for the person who jams the most into a single sentence.

Newspaper writers, supposedly trained in this skill, often overstuff sentences to ridiculous lengths.

So what's wrong with sentence-stuffing? Leaving readability aside for a moment, let's look at how the practice distorts your meaning.

1. Modifying phrases end up too far from the words they modify. They attach to the wrong words, usually with comical results.

2. Cause-and-effect statements misalign, assigning effects to the wrong causes.

3. Pronouns become separated from their antecedents and the reader can't tell who's doing what.

Read this sentence from a local newspaper:

> Police found a resident on a bedroom floor who had fallen and injured herself the day before thanks to a call from an alert neighbor who noted her absence.

You might understand what this sentence generally *means*, but let's take a closer look at what it actually *says*.

Quiz

The correct answers to these questions might surprise you.

Q—Who had fallen and injured herself?
A—The floor.

(… a bedroom floor who had fallen and injured herself…).

Q—What caused the fall?
A—A call from a neighbor.

(… fallen and injured herself the day before thanks to a call from an alert neighbor…).

Q—Where is the neighbor?
A—Not here.

(… an alert neighbor who noted her absence…).

How might the writer have reported the incident more clearly?

> Police found an injured woman on her bedroom floor, where she had fallen the day before. A neighbor, who had not seen the woman all day, called police.

In two sentences, we can express the same thoughts clearly and in the same amount of space.

The next time you're tempted to overstuff a sentence, remember Dolly Parton's famous quip when her gown split at the 1978 Country Music Awards.

> "My daddy said that's what I get for putting fifty pounds of mud in a five-pound bag."

Yes, English
Is Hard

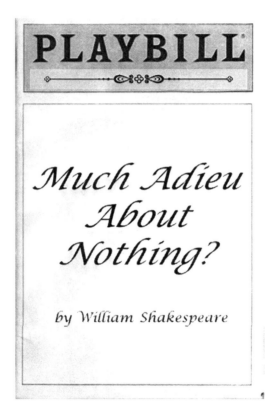

PLAYBILL

Much Adieu About Nothing?

by William Shakespeare

Learning English as a second—or third—language must be incredibly tedious. English has too many irregular verbs, pervasive idioms and slang, inconsistent verb conjugations, inexplicable pronunciations, and spellings that make no sense at all. And, because a majority of Americans have been learning it since birth, we tend to be intolerant of new English learners.

The joke is that many of the least tolerant American critics have poor English mechanics and are terrible spellers. And many immigrants, eager to succeed, have learned proper English remarkably well. But even American-born native English speakers are justifiably vexed by words that sound alike but have different meanings, and spellings that must be memorized one by one because they defy logic. Anyone who thinks Spellcheck or Autocorrect makes it unnecessary to learn to spell deserves what he gets.

Immigrant or native born, sometimes we can do nothing about the frustrating aspects of American English but laugh.

Eluding Trouble
—————— Without Further Ado

Those almost-sound-alike words again. They don't bother most people, just those who want to dress up their writing or sound smart. Nothing wrong with that, as long as you use the correct word. But failing to look it up can make you sound uninformed or—worse—pretentious.

The word *elude* means to avoid or escape, as in "The suspect tried to *elude* the police." But these two words, each similar to *elude*, can get you into trouble.

- allude—to hint or refer to something casually

- exude—to project or radiate

If you use *elude* in place of either of them, the outcome is always bad. The poor reader is supposed to translate, assuming you meant *elude*. Let's suppose your readers can't—or won't—translate, taking you literally instead. What would these sentences mean?

Tiffany denied a liaison with the pool boy, but *eluded* to a friendship with the chauffeur.

(Meaning she *alluded* to it. Tiffany certainly wouldn't avoid it—Tiffany's a tramp.)

The villain was so bad he just *eluded* evil.

(Meaning he *exuded* evil, not avoided it. Then he wouldn't be the villain.)

The other one that always makes me chuckle is:

- ado—a fuss, a flurry of activity

- adieu—French word for goodbye

I doubt that a Shakespeare fan would confuse these two, but that still leaves millions of people who think this is all much ado about nothing. The silliest of all errors is likely to happen when someone thinks that, when in doubt, a French word is always classy.

Please attend to this matter without further *adieu*.

Meaning further *ado*, without fuss. Not that you shouldn't say goodbye anymore.

A recent Internet article on what people drink contained the phrase "Martinis *elude* urban sophistication." My first reaction was to think that the writer meant *exude*. But then I thought, if you drink enough martinis, you'll probably end up acting the opposite of sophisticated. So maybe that's what it meant after all.

Homophones (No, Not That)

This is not about social prejudice, it's about words that sound alike but are spelled differently and have different meanings. I encounter lots of these in editing, and it's clear that many people either carelessly or unknowingly write one thing when they mean another.

Speaking? No problem. After all, they sound alike. But Spellchecker will not find these, and you might not think to look them up.

Suddenly what passes in speech becomes a written communication landmine.

Think, because you don't know the difference, that no one else will? Think again. That's one of the reasons an editor is your first line of defense against embarrassment, especially if you're writing for publication. There are too many of these to cover in one article, but let's start with six pairs I have seen most recently.

- **compliment** (politely express praise)
  complement (add to, complete)

- **forward** (ahead, onward)
  foreword (written piece in the front of a book)

- **manner** (mode of action)
  manor (main house on an estate)

- **speck** (a tiny bit)
  spec (short for speculation or specification)

- **peddle** (sell)
  pedal (ride a bicycle)

- **liable** (likely or apt)
  libel (printed defamation)

The insidious nature of these sound-alike words is that, even if your mind knows which one is correct, your fingers can type the wrong one. I've seen it happen to people who insisted, "I didn't write that!" But they did. At this point, your friend the Spellchecker throws up its hands and announces, "Hey—it's a word. I'm done."

In case there is any lingering doubt about how to use these particular pairs, here is an example paragraph that uses all of them.

> My book was meant to *compliment* the home-building industry and *complement* my other books on construction. I thought a *forward*-looking expert would be a good choice to write the *foreword*. But the expert made statements about a builder who constructs *manor* houses on *spec* in a shady *manner*, and it turns

out there's not a *speck* of truth in the allegations. My publisher has stopped promoting the books and I might have to *pedal* my bike down the street and *peddle* them door to door. I am even *liable* to be accused of *libel*.

By the way, the paragraph is fictional and has no connection to actual persons or events. Just the same, you might want to choose your experts carefully if you ever need a foreword for a book.

Now I Lay Me
Down to Sleep

What were they thinking—the generations of parents who tucked their tots into bed at night with this prayer:

Now I lay me down to sleep, I pray the Lord
my soul to keep.
If I should die before I wake, I pray the Lord
my soul to take.

Pretty heavy stuff for a five-year-old. Sure sweetie, you may not make it through the night, but relax now and go to sleep. Mommy and Daddy need to watch The Voice.

Despite striking terror into the hearts of formerly sleepy children, this verse actually imparts a valuable grammar lesson. Most children grew up confused about *lie* and *lay*, whether they heard this prayer or not. To make it worse, *lay* is the past tense of *lie*. So we're going to straighten this out once and for all. First, let's rule out two definitions: *Lie* as in to tell an untruth, and *lay* as in to have sex. Now that's out of the way and there will be no more snickering. We're talking about these:

- Lie, meaning recline or rest, has no object. You simply lie down.

- Lay, meaning put or place something, has an object. You lay [something] down.

Here is a way to remember the present, past, and past participles of both words:

- Cats lie in the sun. The cat lay there yesterday. She has lain there all day.

- Chickens lay eggs. The crew laid floor tile. He has laid down the rules.

The most unfamiliar word in this group is *lain*. People rarely use it. They say laid instead. That's one of those situations where the correct word sounds awkward or old-fashioned. It's a perfect case for writing around the problem. You could say one of these:

She has been lying there all day.

She has rested there all day.

She lay down this morning and is still there.

Back to the children's prayer, the verb *lay* correctly has an object: *me*. But no one actually says *lay me down*. It's poetry. If grammar were your only concern, you could also say, "Now I lie down to sleep" (no object required) or "Now I lay myself down to sleep" (reflexive object is *myself*). It just wouldn't fit the metric pattern of the verse.

I hope you can rest comfortably now, safe in the knowledge that you know how to use *lie* and *lay*. And if you want to say your prayers, here's a less-scary version.

> Now I lay me down to sleep, I pray the Lord
> my soul to keep.
> Thy love be with me through the night, and
> wake me with the morning light.

Now isn't that better? Sweet dreams.

——————— Confounding Compounds

To make two words out of one, or to make one word out of two? That is often the question. The rule about this is commonly overlooked, especially in instructions.

Even large, monolithic software companies-that-shall-remain-nameless sometimes get it wrong. If good technical writers and editors were valued as much as Autocorrect features you don't want and annoying animated paper clips and cartoon dog assistants you have to turn off... oh well.

The rule, not exclusive to software, is this: An expression formed by a verb and a preposition is spelled as a compound word when used as an adjective or a noun, but must be spelled as two words when used as a verb and a preposition. Notice that it's always two words when describing action. Even if your software screen says otherwise. Are you going to take grammar advice from a cartoon?

In each example, the expression is shown in three forms:

- Adjective (one word)
  Noun (one word)
  Verb-preposition (two words

- You need a *backup* program
  A good *backup* protects your data.
  Be sure to *back up* your system.

- The *login* screen displays first.
  You need credentials to complete the *login*.
  After you *log in*, choose a new password.

- The *signup* sheets are posted.
  Registration requires *signup*.
  Be sure to *sign up* early.

- This is my favorite *makeup* brush.
  The cast uses stage *makeup*.
  It takes thirty minutes to *make up* for a show.

- Our agency says it's a *knockout* idea.
  This commercial is going to be a *knockout*.
  When it airs, we'll *knock out* the competition.

- He dumped her with a *breakup* email.
  What a cowardly way to handle a *breakup*.
  He lacked the courage to *break up* in person.

Remember that software companies are not always right, even the biggest ones. Now you know the rule about these compound words. If you see the rule violated on a computer screen, don't doubt yourself.

When software directions tell you to *startup, login, strikeover, backup, signout,* or *shutdown* (as actions), you can feel smug knowing that each should be two words, not one. It might ease the pain of not buying their software stock back when it was a bargain.

And if you're the scumbag who decided to break up with a girl by email, I hope karma deals you a knockout punch.

Sound-alike Triplets

It's bad enough when two words sound alike but are spelled differently and have different meanings. Those are called homophones. But some homophones have three, or even four, different spellings and meanings.

Some of these result in common mistakes. Others are more obscure, but they're great for making you look good at Scrabble and Jeopardy.

Here are some triplets that sometimes cause funny or embarrassing errors:

- **palate**—roof of the mouth, or a developed taste
  palette—board used by an artist for mixing paint, or a selection of colors
  pallet—holder for stacking goods, made to be moved by a forklift

- **rain**—precipitation, water droplets condensed from atmospheric vapor

reign—ruling or authority, or the time of the dominating power or influence
rein—strap fastened to a bit, used to guide an animal. Control or subdue.

- **auntie**—your parent's sister, affectionately
  anti—against, opposed to
  ante—poker stake collected before cards are dealt to build up a pot

- **hoard**—collection of objects, often secretly or compulsively saved to excess
  horde—a multitude, mass, or crowd
  [let's hope you don't have to use this one]—compromised one's principles for personal gain; prostituted

And here they are, used in sentences:

Jeremy's educated *palate*, and his appreciation for a rainbow *palette* of wines, led him to order an entire *pallet* of the new reds for his restaurant.

Unseasonal *rain* during the *reign* of the young king left him no choice but to *rein* in the eager army and postpone the attack.

Auntie Grace, though publicly *anti*-gambling, was always ready to *ante* up on girls' poker night.

As the *horde* of eager would-be starlets flocked to Hollywood, trying to *hoard* every dollar they could, some waited tables, some worked in offices, and some [compromised] their way into films.

C'mon—you didn't really expect me to say that, did you?

—————————— A Cautionery Tale

Yes, I know it's misspelled. This is about words that some people spell with—ary, but shouldn't. *Cautionary* is one that does end in—ary.

The next time you're browsing in a quaint European village, admiring the local stationery, stitchery, or confectionery, touring a monastery with a stone-walled cemetery, remember: That wall is not made of masonary. In fact, there is no such word as *masonary*, despite what the tradesman building your stone wall might argue. The word is *masonry*. Three syllables, not four.

It's possible that the guy stringing the barbed wire on your ranch calls it bob wire too (another topic), but that doesn't make it correct.

This commentary might make me an adversary to some who don't know an aviary from an apiary, but, though opinions vary and I'm hardly a literary luminary, my thoughts are far from arbitrary. And anyway, your participation is strictly voluntary.

If we discount masonary, which has an added letter, making it a non-word, I've recently seen these four words misspelled—in print—or on the Internet (which almost doesn't count).

- monastary (instead of monastery

- confectionary (instead of confectionery)

- cemetary (instead of cemetery)

- stationary (instead of stationery)

In defense of the last one, *stationary* is at least a real word. It means fixed, not moving. But if it's writing paper you want, it's *stationery*. Those two can be confusing. The other three aren't even in the dictionery—I mean, dictionary.

My goal here is not to debate the fine points of grammar. So-called experts disagree on rules and whether common usage should drive acceptance. But I weigh in when nonstandard constructions or spellings misdirect what you're trying to communicate. If there's an—ery where there should be an—ary (or the reverse), it's either misleading or distracting, or both.

Words ending in—ary are most often adjectives, although they can also be nouns. Words ending in—ery are usually nouns, but you can't depend on that as a rule either.

Writing is a solitary pursuit. But if you have an ordinary vocabulary, don't suffer an imaginary coronary. Take a temporary, momentary break. Search your online library or dictionary.

Just remember that language can be fluxionary, but spelling is necessary, so be wary.

Scary? Very.

Almost-Homophones
for Smart People

The world is full of people who mangle the English language and many of them don't even want help. My concern is smart people who just need a few reminders now and then. I always hope these people will see the humor in it, but sometimes they don't.

People in the public eye, news reporters, business leaders, role models— these people have a responsibility to set a good example, don't they? But many word pairs are so close that even professional communicators confuse them.

Almost every day I read or hear some example of intelligent, professional people gone ever-so-slightly astray. Just enough to be wrong. I wince every time I see or hear one of these:

- It's a mute point.

- What have we got to loose?

- To error is human...

- That's just not my for-tay.

A couple of the pronunciations in this list of reminders might surprise you. They're in this format: **word** (pronunciation)—meaning.

- **moot** *(moot)*—open to debate
  mute *(myoot)*—silent or unable to speak

- **lose** *(looz)*—to misplace or to fail
  loose *(luce)*—free from restraint, not bound

- **error** *(air-or)*—a mistake
  err *(urr, not air)*—to make a mistake

- **fort** *(fort)*—a strong place used for protection
  forte *(fort, not for-tay unless used as a musical term)*—a talent or skill

Few people would correctly articulate "To err *(urr)* is human." It's one of those phrases that's OK to write, but people would look at you oddly if you said it properly. Unless, of course, they were academics or literature buffs. If that's your audience, do it and impress them. The other one is *forte*. If you're a musician, *for-tay* means loud. But if you're talking about your strengths, it is correctly pronounced *fort*. Again, choose your audience.

At the height of Michael Jackson's career, the word *androgynous* was all over radio and TV. It described the cross-gender look of entertainers like Jackson, David Bowie, and k.d.lang. It was the favorite buzzword of fashion critics and newscasters, and they loved to say it. One day I heard a radio announcer say, "On the highway north of town, a tanker truck has just overturned, spilling thirty thousand gallons of androgynous ammonia..."

I wrote a letter to the radio station and thanked them for the report, saying, "As frightening as a spill of *anhydrous* ammonia would have been, just imagine the danger of thirty thousand gallons of hermaphroditic gas wandering around in search of a gender preference."

They did not reply, of course. I think they were not amused. Oh well, to err is human.

Beg Pardons, Not Questions

Certain words and expressions pop up mostly when people are trying, too hard, to sound intelligent. The unconsciously ungrammatical don't care, so they don't try. But others, in an attempt to show how smart they are, show exactly the opposite.

Intellectuals in TV interviews and in print are fond of misusing the phrase *it begs the question*.

Incorrect example

> "Television commentators and newspaper columnists reach large, and sometimes critical, audiences. Their every grammatical mistake is exposed. It begs the question, why don't they look things up?"

So why is that wrong? Because this common misuse means it raises the question.

It begs the question refers to a logical fallacy in which a statement refers to its own assertion to prove the assertion. It's a bit like a tautological or circular argument, but not exactly.

Here's an easy way to tell which is correct. If the expression is followed by the actual question, use *raises* instead of *begs*. "It raises the question, why don't they look things up?"

Correct example

> Me: Although Miss Hereford won the pageant, the judging was unfair because Miss Holstein was the prettiest.
>
> You: That begs the question.

The assertion that Miss H was the prettiest is subjective, and does not prove that the judging was unfair. The proof of the conclusion relies on its own unprovable premise.

In the dark underworld of grammar geeks, you can find message boards, websites, and even paraphernalia devoted to the correct use of BTQ (begs the question). You can order T-shirts, coffee mugs, and even thongs emblazoned with the logo and explanation of BTQ. You can download and print cards to hand out to people who misuse it—somewhat like a citizen's arrest, I guess. Imagine what fun it must be to lie in wait, hoping someone will say it, so you can pounce with your little cards.

Ha!

I don't want to know how wearing a BTQ thong proves your dedication or helps to evangelize the point. And the idea of the grammar police at a party with a pocket full of BTQ cards, wearing a thong, just isn't an image I want in my head.

Nothing good comes from citizen's arrests anyway. The offenders won't heed the message. They will, however, remember that you're a pompous know-it-all and they want to be as far away from you as possible.

Begs the question is so widely misused that people will probably misunderstand if you use it correctly. Just as, in cooking directions, you would not say this:

> Melt some butter in a pan. About one convex polyhedron bounded by six quadrilateral faces should be enough.

Yes, it's true that butter does not come in cubes, despite what people call them. But an unfamiliar—though technically correct—phrase is guaranteed to stop communication dead in its tracks.

So do all ye guardians of the language just give up? Never. My advice is to avoid even the correct usage of BTQ unless you're addressing an audience made up entirely of lawyers, philosophers, logic professors, or grammar geeks. For heaven's sake, don't go around handing out BTQ cards, and just call it a stick of butter.

But if you believe it's OK to use the expression *begs the question* incorrectly because everyone does it anyway and no one knows the difference...

... now that begs the question.

The Mother Load

In just one week, I've seen two smart people use the expression *mother load* in reference to a large amount of something. I've also seen it used in a book by one not-so-smart writer, and overlooked by a sleepy editor.

Listen up, folks, it's *mother lode*. L-O-D-E. The term, from the mining industry, refers to a major deposit of gold or silver ore. It is also used to describe something valuable or in great abundance, and that's where people get into trouble. Perhaps it suggests the idea of *mother of all loads*, but that's neither its origin nor its current meaning.

There is only one way the term *mother load* makes any sense. Imagine a mythical family in which each member is assigned a separate basket of laundry to wash, dry, and fold. You know the family is mythical because the children are actually doing laundry.

The family responsibilities are these:

- Father—his own T-shirts, shorts, underwear, socks, and pajamas

- Son—his own T-shirts, shorts, underwear, socks, and pajamas

- Daughter—her own T-shirts, shorts, underwear, socks, and pajamas

- Mother—her own T-shirts, shorts, underwear, socks, and pajamas, anything that requires special handling, jeans, skirts, dresses, blouses, slip covers, curtains, school uniforms, soccer uniforms, ballet tutus, Halloween costumes, choir robes, sheets, workout clothes, yoga clothes, pillowcases, blankets, bath towels, hand towels, tea towels, kitchen towels, beach towels, tablecloths, napkins, bathmats, dusting cloths, patio cushions, and the dog bed.

In the sense that the *mother load* is the largest, the term is appropriate here.

So feel free to use it, but only if you're writing about laundry.

Genteel or Gentile?

Nowadays, most civilized people try not to offend entire groups—genders, races, or religions. Those who do so on purpose are considered boorish and unenlightened, right?

But sometimes the well-intentioned are also clueless about these two words. It's easy to offend without meaning to, and that's what we want to prevent here.

Here's the scoop:

- Gentile (pronounced JEN-tyle) means non-Jewish.

- genteel (pronounced jen-TEEL) means polite, well-mannered, or refined.

See the problem? You try to say something nice about a person's manners but instead you imply a religious connection that's not there, excluding an entire group of people. This is what the British call a sticky wicket.

You've no doubt seen those tiresome postcard-type memes in decorative fonts that people post on LinkedIn, Facebook, or Twitter because they can't think of anything original to say. They are calculated to elicit such comments as Hilarious! or So True! One shows a vintage drawing of an 1890s woman with this text:

> All spring and summer she was a gentile Southern lady. Then football season started...

So what's wrong with that? Let me count the ways. Gentile, when used correctly, is capitalized and its very definition is exclusionary. The hilarious postcard quote literally says the lady was not Jewish. The word they should have used here is *genteel*. Even in the South, religion has nothing to do with one's manners or enthusiasm for football. Picture a Jewish woman in a Florida State jersey demanding, "So what am I—chopped liver?"

Jews are not likely to mix up these two words, so I'm probably preaching to Gentiles here. If you are one, repeat after me:

- Gentile is capitalized.

- Genteel is not, unless it's the first word in a sentence like this one.

- Gentiles (non-Jews) can be genteel, but they can also be boorish and rude.

- Genteel (polite, refined) people can be either Jewish or non-Jewish. That includes pretty much everyone.

Got it? Mazel Tov!

————— All My Exes

do not live in Texas, as appealing as the country song makes that sound. But I am vexed, perplexed, and exasperated by people who feel compelled to put an X where it doesn't belong. Most of the time there's an S involved, and the perpetrators seem unable to tell the difference between them.

The sound made by the letter X is a combination of two other letter sounds—K and S. If you're a small child or an adult just learning English, it's understandable, and even cute, that you might reverse them. But the grace period on that one expires at about age five, at least for native English speakers.

Whenever I hear someone pronounce *ask* with an X instead of an SK sound, I imagine Lizzie Borden saying, "Papa, may I go to Abigail's party?" That's when he says—wait for it— "Go axe your mother."

Regardless of how carelessly we pronounce words, the act of writing them down requires more caution. There it is in print, and no one can be accused of hearing it incorrectly.

So beware of these words that are neither pronounced nor spelled with an X:

- Excalate
  It's *escalate*. A back-formation from *escalator*, derived from a Latin word (scalae) meaning a flight of steps. But enough of that.

- Excape
  Should be *escape*. Not something Superman used to wear.

- Expecially
  The word is *especially*. You don't say *xpecial*, do you?

- Excetera
  From two Latin words, *et cetera*. There's not even an S in this one.

- Expresso
  There is no X in the Italian alphabet, and none in your coffee. It's *espresso*.

Now that you know the exact spellings, there's no need to expound, expand the explanation, experience exhaustion, exhibit expertise, or explain extra examples, is there?

Excellent.

To E or Not To E

An error lurks in each of these sentences. How many can you find?

- Surely you don't think his story is believeable.

- Hurricanes can be disasterous.

- Flowers—what a lovely rememberance.

- A good manager lets you work without hinderance.

- Tactics like that will never win an arguement.

- Well that's an unexpected developement.

- Thunder is usually preceded by lightening.

The last word in each sentence contains an extra letter e. Several are understandable. All are variations of a root word, and that's where the problem lies.

In these words, an e in the original word is dropped when it becomes an adjective:

- believe -> believable

- disaster -> disastrous

In these three, an e is dropped when the root word becomes a noun:

- remember->remembrance

- hinder->hindrance

- argue->argument

I have no explanation for *developement* instead of *development*. The root word is develop, not develope. Maybe people are thinking of *envelope*? Maybe it's just easy to hit the e key when you're typing. Whatever the reason, I see that one often.

Lightening is a legitimate word. It just doesn't mean electro-static discharge visible as jagged steaks of light in the sky, followed by thunder. It refers to reducing weight or color intensity. You *lighten* a load or *lighten* a color. So leave out the e if you're talking about something that happens in an electrical storm.

But be sure to add the e if you text your stylist and arrange to have it done to a few streaks in your hair.

Verses Versus Versus

They're at it again—smart people who confuse similar-sounding words. Spellchecker tells you they're correctly spelled, but can't tell you how to use them.

In an article about a company's accounting woes, I saw this phrase:

They could have prevented the disparage...

OK, class, *disparage* is a verb. It means to speak negatively about someone or something. In slang terms, to disparage means to bad-mouth. In any case, it cannot function as the direct object of the verb *prevented*.

The word this writer was going for is *disparity*. It is a noun, and it has nothing to do with bad-mouthing. It means difference. In the article, it was clear that the writer meant the funds reported from two sources did not match. It would have been appropriate to *disparage* whoever was responsible for the *disparity*.

An otherwise informative article discussed the merits of various seat choices on airplanes.

Some people prefer an isle seat...

Isle is a shortened, somewhat poetic form of *island*. As in The Isle of Capri or Ireland, the Emerald Isle. Better to be in either of those places than stuck on an airplane in any seat. That narrow passage where they push the food carts and whack your elbows is the aisle.

I almost hesitate to include sports writers in the smart people category, although there are many smart sports writers. Sadly, some were hired for their subject knowledge despite their abysmal use of English. In a field where face-offs are common, team against team, individual against individual, or individual against record, you'd think this one would never occur. But it does:

> Next week's matchup features the Angels verses the Red Sox...

Unless the contest requires baseball players to go head-to-head in a freestyle rap competition, spontaneously spouting rhyming couplets, they mean versus.

Versus comes from Latin, and it means against, or opposed to. It can be spelled out or abbreviated either vs or v (in legal usage, with or without periods after). As in Angels versus Red Sox, Marbury vs. Madison, or Roe v Wade.

> Some errors just drive me to curses
> All tact and decorum disperses.
> > There's you're and there's your,
> > Two, to, too and more,
> And don't forget versus v. verses.

Old Words, New Tech

Today's children probably wonder about some of the technical terms we use. Names for obsolete technology somehow manage to stick around long after their antecedents lie, refusing to decompose, in a landfill.

When applied to the new technology that took its place, the old name requires some explanation. At least people finally stopped referring to removable storage media as floppy disks. I last saw a five-and-a-quarter-inch flexible disk in about 1989, but the term persisted long after disks had long ceased to be floppy.

If you've been around small children lately, you're probably amazed at how tech-savvy they are. The little rug-rats are clever all right, but they don't know everything. They need us to explain many things. Why we use certain terms. Where those words came from. Why we wore orange polyester in the seventies… but I digress.

Current examples include:

- Pick up the phone, hang up the phone, or dial the number

  How many kids have ever used a phone you can pick up, hang up, or dial?

- Answering machine picks up on the fourth ring

  There is no physical machine, and the phone plays a digitally recorded tone, or even a popular song. No bell, no ringing. Although the ringtone might be a digital recording of an old-fashioned phone ringing. No wonder they're confused.

- Cc: line in email

  Carbon copy. Yes, years ago, we made physical copies on a typewriter with this nasty coated paper that rubbed off on your fingers, clothes, and other pages. No, really. We did. So what does that have to do with email?

- Stay home and watch the tube.

  How long has it been since televisions had tubes of any kind?

- Tape your favorite TV show

  Older children might remember the VCR, but most have experienced only digital recording. So when they hear this phrase, they might wonder where the tape is. It's like magic, and it's invisible, somewhere inside the TV. Or some other device. Anyway, there's nothing to snarl, tangle, rewind, label, or store in boxes.

Here's an assignment:

Just for fun, find an eight-year-old and try to explain why we still say:

- The accident was filmed by a witness with a cell phone.

- Roll down your car window.

- That singer has her own label.

- Her husband owns a record company.

- On the home screen, click one of the radio buttons.

- My motorcycle has a three hundred horsepower engine.

Seriously, Daddy... *HORSE*... power?

Tense Moments

I admire those who try to teach English to people who already speak and write another language. It's hard enough to write English on a blank slate, so to speak, when a child is young and doesn't know much yet.

But if the students are intelligent adults, fluent in another language, their questions might be unanswerable.

OK class, today we're going to study these six verbs, their spellings, and their past tense forms.

1. lead

    Present—*Lead*, follow, or get out of the way.

    Past—The winning float *led* the parade.

2. bleed

    Present—Facial lacerations often *bleed* profusely.

    Past—The victim *bled* from his head wounds.

3. breed

Present—The rancher decided to *breed* livestock.

Past—He *bred* prize-winning cattle.

4. read

Present—I like to *read* the classics.

Past—I *read* that one in school years ago.

5. plead

Present—How does the defendant *plead*?

Past—When I *pleaded* with him, he *pled* guilty.

6. speed

Present—It's illegal to *speed* in a school zone

Past—The suspect *sped* through a school zone, and then *speeded* away in a van.

Any questions? Yes—you in the back...

Q—If the past tense of lead is led, what is that stuff in my pencil (lead)?

Q—If lead is spelled with an a in it, why isn't bleed spelled blead?

Q—If you put an a in breed instead of just taking an e out, why does it make bread (as in a sandwich) that sounds like bred?

Q—Why is the past tense of read spelled the same but pronounced red, while reed is an entirely different word?

Q—Why is there no pleed, but both pleaded and pled are OK? Why don't we say readed?

Q—Don't tell me—there's no spead, is there? It's just like plead only completely different?

Gosh, would you look at the time! I wish I could answer all of your excellent questions, but the bell is going to ring soon.

Here's next week's assignment. Read the section that discusses why, if you used the gh sound in *rough*, the o sound in *women*, and the ti sound in *action*, the word *fish* should be spelled *ghoti*.

Class dismissed.

Stick out Your Tongue and Say, "Phtht!"

This is something like a smart person's spelling bee, only there are no prizes. These are words almost no one pronounces correctly, and even fewer spell correctly.

College professors, worldly and sophisticated people, even medical doctors have argued with me on the spelling and pronunciation of these words (bad mistake). I'm not dumb enough to discuss spelling unless I've looked it up first.

The common problem with all of these words is a *ph* somewhere in the middle that everyone assumes is just a *p*.

Here are the right and wrong spellings, and pronunciations, of six tricky words:

1. amphitheater (AM-fa-thee-a-tur)

   Not ampitheater (AM-pa-thee-a-tur)

2. diphtheria (dif-THEER-ee-a)

   Not diptheria (dip-THEER-ee-a)

3. diphthong (DIF-thong)

   Not dipthong (DIP-thong)

4. naphtha (NAF-tha)

   Not naptha (NAP-tha)

5. ophthalmologist (ahf-thal-MOL-o-jist)

   Not opthamologist (op-tha-MOL-o-jist)

6. pamphlet (PAM-flet)

   Not pamplet (PAM-plet)

Those of you who are feeling smug, now, tell the truth. Did you know about the extra *l* in ophthalmologist? That would be worth bonus points if we were keeping score. These are examples of words we've spoken and perhaps written for years without noticing those little surprises lurking among the consonants.

Something about them tricks the eye and they blend right in. It's hard to get your tongue and teeth to say ophthalmologist and diphtheria. Although if you were in need of the former and wanted an immunization against the latter, I doubt you'd care how they were pronounced.

I hate to contribute to even more boring cocktail conversation, but if you run out of things to say, you can always sashay up to someone and say, "Hi! Did you know that the word *amphitheater* is actually spelled..." You might be the instant life of the party. Let me know if that works for you. If it does, you need to go to better parties.

No one is going to shun you if you mispronounce these words, because they are so rarely said correctly. But you might score a scholarship if you could sneak into a spelling bee disguised as a twelve-year-old.

Not To Be
—————Taken Literally

Colorful language, idioms, and folk sayings are part of the stew that is American English. When you use words figuratively, you open a Pandora's box of potential for misunderstanding (see what I did there?).

Idioms and other figurative references are often regional or generational. An expression your Alabama grandma used might mean something quite different to your Brooklyn-born nephew. Or it might just produce a blank stare.

People hear colloquialisms for decades and repeat them, never bothering to check their origins or even their meanings. Put them to music and you have a whole new world of comedic possibilities.

Ironic—Literally Surreal

When you use one of these three words to add emphasis or credibility to a statement, it might well have the opposite effect. Why? Because they're used incorrectly so often that few people take them seriously. They can make you sound immature and silly.

Just ask Alanis Morissette. In 1996 she released a song called *Ironic*. It describes a number of negative events and repeatedly asks the question:

Isn't it ironic? Don't you think?

An army of grammar police rose up to condemn, ridicule, and parody the song. The situations in the song, you see, were not all truly ironic.

One of Morissette's non-ironies was *A black fly in your chardonnay*. Another was *Rain on your wedding day*. Critics blasted her because both of these situations are merely unfortunate. Ironic means happening in a way that is opposite from what is expected, and usually causing wry amusement. A bit of bad luck or a mere coincidence does not qualify as ironic.

When people say *literally* for emphasis, they usually mean *figuratively*—just the opposite:

> It was so funny I literally split my sides laughing.

> So... did you go to the hospital? Was it painful? Did you have stitches?

The third overused word is *surreal*, as in:

> We were both wearing the same dress. It was so surreal.

Surreal seems to need a modifier—*so*—to add weight to the statement. Apparently surreal (weird, bizarre, having the qualities of a dream) is not strong enough by itself. In any case, showing up at a party in a dress identical to that of another guest is awkward, but hardly a nightmare.

All three of these words, used singly or in combination, imply exaggeration. They alert your audience to activate the BS filter and prepare to question what you're saying.

So if you say, "I literally fell down laughing," you'd better be describing a loss of balance ending with you on the floor. And if you were seeing melting clocks and a giraffe aflame, you could correctly describe it as surreal. Rain on your wedding day could be ironic... if you were marrying a TV meteorologist who had promised sunny weather. On the air.

But a black fly in your chardonnay? That's just disgusting.

Misheard Melodies and
Mangled Metaphors

Misunderstood song lyrics are common, given the lack of enunciation in much vocal music. Although Billy Joel sang, "You may be right, I may be crazy," some people heard, "You made the rice, I made the gravy"

The Monkees sang, "Then I saw her face, now I'm a believer," and some heard, "Then I saw her face, now I'm gonna leave her."

The classic example is the generations of kids who think the Beatles were singing, "Hey, dude" [sigh].

Old figures of speech suffer the same fate when people repeat them in conversation for years, and then they want to write them down. Hilarious misinterpretations of these phrases might pass in a speech if the audience already likes you. But please, please don't use them in writing. The origins of many such clichés are long forgotten, so the phrase makes no sense at all. Here are some examples:

- pink (or white) elephant in the room (elephant in the room)

A pink elephant is a drink-induced hallucination. A white elephant is some useless thing you don't want. But an elephant in the room is an awkward subject no one wants to talk about.

- not my strong suit of clothes (not my strong suit)

This refers to the suits of playing cards–clubs, spades, diamonds, or hearts. It has nothing to do with apparel.

- talking off the same sheet of music (playing off the same sheet of music)

Reading from the same page? Script? Maybe, but you play or at least sing off the same sheet of music.

- long road to hoe (long row to hoe)

Attacking pavement with a garden tool sounds like frustrating work. Refers to chopping weeds from a row of crops, not a road.

- this isn't set into stone (set in concrete, carved into stone)

Tricky. Correctly, you set things in concrete or carve them into stone. Lots of people get this one wrong.

The best plan is to choose better ways to illustrate what you want to say. Figurative language can be colloquial, hackneyed, and tiresome. If it's an old expression you've heard all your life, there is always the danger that you, your fifth grade teacher, and everyone in your neighborhood has been saying it wrong all these years.

And remember that, despite what you might have heard, Bob Dylan did not write, "The ants are my friends, they're blowin' in the wind."

The Game of Gossip

Remember the old childhood game called Gossip or Telephone? A whispered phrase was passed from one party guest to another. The object was to see how that phrase had changed by the time it got to the last person. *Going to the dance* turned into *Glowing doo-doo France* and hilarity ensued.

This game teaches us that it's risky to repeat expressions you only think you've heard correctly—especially if you don't quite know what they mean. Here are three commonly mangled expressions I've heard recently:

Chalk-full

It's *chock-full*. Its origin, from middle English, is obscure. But it means full to the limit, at capacity. It has nothing to do with those sticks of calcium sulfate they used in schools before whiteboards were invented.

Half-mask

As in, *His pants were at half-mask*. The expression *half-mast*, refers to lowering a flag to honor a person or event. That's the meaning that applies to baggy trousers. A half-mask is what the guy in Phantom of the Opera wears on his face.

Ying and yang

The complementary forces in Chinese philosophy are *yin* (no g) and *yang*. Ying and Yang sound like cute names for twin pandas, though.

You've probably heard someone use at least one of these phrases incorrectly. Well if that person jumped off a bridge, would you jump off too? Don't be the person who passes it on, perpetuating the mistake. Before you repeat some idiom you've only heard, look it up in print or verify its meaning. And, no, print on Twitter, Facebook, or an Internet discussion group does not count. That's where English goes to die.

The game of Gossip is fun for children's birthday parties. But when you're all grown up and people laugh because you've said chalk-full, half-mask, or ying and yang, they're not having fun, they're making fun.

And if they're making fun because you wear your pants at half-mast, you're on your own.

The Kid Gloves Are Off

Want a job, promotion, business success? Just search the Internet, that bottomless vat of guidance. Advice for savvy people, not idiots who would wear flip-flops to a job interview. Cuff links, neckties, necklines, hem lengths, projecting just the right image... as if these superficial details give you a secret advantage in the workplace.

You'll find job-hunting tips, interview techniques, and negotiating tactics. What to say and how to respond with poise under stress. Everyone knows that sloppy clothes and a surly attitude hurt you. But neither the right suit nor an arsenal of smooth replies will get you hired or promoted. They say, at most, "I look pleasant and I'm well prepared."

So what else is there? Hiring and promoting managers want you to be smart, and no seminar or list of Top Ten anything can deliver that. Unless you present multiple advanced degrees in some impressive field, it's a perception that's difficult to build—and easy to destroy—in a few seconds.

On the job, you establish a pattern of wise decisions, display good judgment, and show your communication skills over time. If you're looking for a job, you make sure your résumé is free of spelling and grammatical errors. Most of all, don't overlook your online persona. It's all out there and searchable by current or prospective employers.

If you communicate through email, messaging, LinkedIn, Twitter, Facebook, Instagram, and even corporate web sites, here's a tip:

Some writing mistakes make people think you are stupid.

There, I've said it. I'm sorry if it sounds judgmental, but it's meant to help you avoid embarrassment. Smart takes time to build, but stupid can occur in an instant. Everyone makes little mistakes now and then. But, to many people, certain kinds of blunders qualify as ignorant errors. These are not typos made in haste. They are gaffes that imply you don't know any better.

Ignorant errors include using the wrong word, misspelling words you should have learned in elementary school, and misquoting idioms. Here are three examples I've seen just today in postings from supposedly reputable business sources:

- We have nothing to loose.

    OK, one more time, the word you want here is *lose*. The next time you're tempted to type *loose*, remember that it rhymes with goose, noose, and caboose. Is that really the word you want to use? (*Use* rhymes with *lose*.)

- Alright stop.

  I don't care if you've seen this one in TV commercials or on Facebook or in song lyrics. It's wrong. *Almost, already,* and *altogether* are words. But there is no such word as *alright.* It's *all right.* Always.

- Handle them with kit gloves.

  The expression *kid gloves* refers to treating something carefully or delicately. It comes from elegant eighteenth-century white dress gloves made of soft leather, the skin of young goats or lambs (kids). Nothing remotely connected with the word *kit.*

Go ahead. Argue that most people don't know the difference or that they shouldn't judge you by such things. The same could be said of those sharp business outfits and interview training. But many people do know and care, and all it takes is one of them. One who reads your social media post and blasts you in a comment. Or laughs at your email sales pitch and doesn't call you back. Or scans your résumé and doesn't hire you. No one seems to wear kid gloves anymore.

The instant, faceless nature of online interaction lends itself to vicious attacks. Mean-spirited snipers lurk in dark Internet caves. Their criticism can be brutal, and it seems to last forever in cyberspace. So take care. There be grammar trolls.

Animal Idioms

No animals were harmed in the creation of this article, but the English language sustained a few minor abrasions and contusions. A common type of idiom attributes an animal quality to humans:

Strong as an ox

Proud as a peacock

Gentle as a lamb

Those are easy to understand and difficult to mess up. No one is likely to say strong as a lamb, proud as an ox, or gentle as a peacock. If you had ever encountered an enraged peacock, you'd understand.

Other expressions make me wonder if the writer has ever even seen a farm animal. I've seen all three of these in print:

- Bull in a china closet

The original expression, *bull in a china shop*, describes someone whose violent or clumsy behavior damages everything around him. In defense of bulls everywhere, it's conceivable that you might lead a docile bovine through a china shop without chipping a single teacup. But I'd like to see you stuff one into a china closet.

- They needed an escape goat

  This atrocity happens when people hear the (legitimate) word *scapegoat* and think someone is talking about a Houdini-like domesticated ruminant. A scapegoat (no e) is a person who gets blamed for someone else's misdeeds. In politics, for example, when a policy or program fails, the responsible parties and the media often select a scapegoat to take the criticism.

- Till the cows come home to roost

  This one is a mixture of two concepts. *Till the cows come home* refers to the practice of turning cows out to pasture in the morning, and then bringing them into the barnyard for the night. In other words, all day. If you say "I'll be working on this project till the cows come home," you just mean for a long time.

  The roost part comes from the expression *chickens will come home to roost*. That refers to a moment of accountability when past sins or omissions must be acknowledged and perhaps punished.

Only a city slicker would suggest a scenario in which a twelve hundred-pound, four-legged creature with cloven hooves would perch daintily on a narrow shelf.

The chickens would be annoyed, but it would make a great YouTube video.

Beyond the Pail

When mispronounced or misspelled, many common words and expressions suggest silly mental pictures that can help you to remember the right way to say or spell them. Here are three of my favorite examples:

- beyond the pail (instead of beyond the pale)

The correct version, *beyond the pale*, originated centuries ago in Europe and referred to an actual fence or implied boundary (The Pale) around an area of land controlled by ruling forces. Areas outside—or beyond—The Pale were considered hostile or dangerous territory. The expression now means outside the boundaries of accepted, or civilized, behavior. At no time in history were buckets involved.

- wreckless driving (instead of reckless driving)

Reckless (without the w) describes a situation in which a driver disregards the rules, behaving carelessly and irresponsibly behind the wheel. Reckless drivers often cause accidents. A reckless driver is probably not wreckless for long. A wreckless driver (with a w) has no accidents and is the opposite of reckless.

- half-hazard (instead of haphazard)

The correct word, *haphazard*, means unplanned, irregular, or random. Aimless, dependent on chance. If you're tempted to say or spell *half-hazard*, just picture one of these:

Remember that,unless they describe one of these pictures, wreckless and half-hazard are beyond the pale.

Borrowing from
—————Other Languages

merican English didn't spring, fully formed, from some eighteenth-century meeting of the Continental Congress. It evolved slowly from multiple sources, rich with the influences of diverse cultures. Common words we use every day have their origins in France, Greece, Italy, or ancient Rome. We anglicize their pronunciations, often badly, and use them incorrectly in sentences.

We sometimes (dare I say it?) put on airs and spring French words on unsuspecting bystanders. Or we try to make our writing seem academic with Latin abbreviations, more often incorrectly abbreviated and punctuated than not.

Trouble is, the off-chance that the attempt will impress some-one is not worth the risk that someone else will recognize the blunder and think you're a pompous fool.

————————— French Revolution

To sound classy, (as anyone who uses that word to describe himself clearly is not), drop a few French words into the conversation. To sound ignorant, drop in a horribly mispronounced French word.

But to sound completely stupid, use a couple of nonsense syllables that started out French and mutated into American Hillbilly.

Well-meaning Americans can be excused for not getting French pronunciations quite right. French has entirely too many silent letters, and the vowel sounds feel uncomfortable in our mouths. The best most of us can do is try.

So here are two popular menu items anyone can say:

> crème brûlée—KREMM broo-LAY (not KREEM broo-LAY)

The *crème* rhymes with stem, not steam. Here's another:

crêpes—KREPPS (not KRAPES)

Rhymes with steps, not grapes.

Mispronouncing is one thing, but writing is another. It's bad enough when speakers pronounce these next examples. When people actually write them, it's inexcusable:

Wa-la!

Used in a moment of revelation. Beat the egg whites until stiff, and—wa-la! Meringue!

When pronounced, it sounds close to *Voila!* But every time someone writes it, Inspector Clouseau spins in his grave. Oh—and notice that it's V-O-I-L-A, not V-I-O-L-A (a viola is a stringed instrument similar to a violin).

My personal favorite is:

Boo-coo

Most often followed by buck*s*. As in "Man, that musta cost boo-coo bucks."

A few people might have started this in fun, intentionally mispronouncing *beaucoup* (it rhymes with GO TO, not cuckoo) but it's become common among speakers and writers who have no idea where it originated.

Let's just fix this once and for all. For those determined to mangle French words (while insisting that everyone else should speak English, dammit), here are some easier substitutes:

Instead of this ...	Say this
crème brûlée	puddin'
crêpes	pancakes
Voila!	Dang!
beaucoup	whole bunch

——————————————— Et Tu, Brute?

Want your writing to seem academic? Scholarly? More intelligent? Think twice before sprinkling it with Latin phrases or abbreviations.

Warning: Latin is dangerous. Unless you've read the instruction manual carefully, it can cause headaches, dizziness, condescension, accusations of silliness, and personal humiliation.

To be clear, the academic world is an appropriate place for Latin, correctly used and abbreviated. Here, we're talking about general and business communication. If you read "That statement is a non sequester," chances are the writer meant *non sequitur* (an argument whose conclusion does not follow from what preceded it).

Even if you don't care about appearing pretentious, let's look at the practical reasons for caution. In business these days, it's likely that much of your audience speaks English as a second, or third, language. Never mind Latin.

If you work for an international company, your writing might have to be translated for global distribution. Translation software is easily confused by Latin mixed with English expressions, abbreviated or not. The results can be hilarious, but not at all what you meant to say.

Check out this list of common Latinisms, the problems they cause, and what you might say instead:

- etc.

  Et cetera. Often misspelled *ect* or with no period. Often the last word in the sentence, so one period or two? Just say *and so on.*

- et al.

  Et alii, or et aliae. Only the second word gets a period. Just say *and others.*

- e.g.

  Exempli gratia. Each letter gets a period. Just say *for example.*

- i.e.

  Id est. Each letter gets a period. Just say *that is.*

- errata

  Plural of erratum. Just say *errors.*

- via

  Just plain pretentious. Say *by* or *through*.

- a criteria

  It's plural. One *criterion*, two *criteria*.

- a phenomena

  It's plural. One *phenomenon*, two *phenomena*.

- *alumna

  Singular form, feminine. One *alumna*, two *alumnae*.

- *alumnus

  Singular form, masculine. One *alumnus*, two *alumni*.

*What if your reference is a co-ed institution or you're not comfortable with the whole alumna/alumnae, alumnus/alumni question? If the situation is casual, call them alums. If not, call them graduates.

General understanding and translation software are reasons enough to avoid these Latin traps, but closed-captioning for speech and narration makes it hopeless. Non-human interpreters have enough trouble with simple English. Let's not confuse them further.

My favorite mangled Latinism is the mélange infortunatus of Latin and French, a sort of double whammy of pretentiousness. If you insist on spouting Latin, just be sure to say *persona non grata*, not *persona au gratin*. Unless you really do mean someone who's covered with baked breadcrumbs and cheese.

—————————————— Zut Alors!

I'll be the first to admit it. I don't speak French. I do know how to say, "I'm sorry, I don't speak French very well." But that usually brings an unintelligible rapid-fire response— in French. Maybe I should learn to say it in German.

The French have taken a lot of abuse from American comedians, so it must be secretly satisfying to them when one of us mangles a French phrase while trying to sound sophisticated and worldly. Many Europeans already think we're clumsy and ill-mannered, and sometimes they are right. But often, we just don't know any better.

Always ask yourself whether your goal is to communicate or to impress. Peppering your writing with French phrases is an embarrassment waiting to happen. French is full of silent letters, accent marks, and gender-specific pronouns. And the people you want most to impress are the least likely to forgive a failed attempt.

Now don't get me wrong—if you speak and spell flawless French, or if it's part of your character and suits your subject, go for it. Otherwise, consult some reliable reference before venturing out into this treacherous territory. Spare yourself these indignities:

- bon appetite (it's *bon appetit*)

- Viola! (for *Voila!* A viola is a stringed instrument.)

- visa vie (for *vis-à-vis*)

- au contrair **or au contrary** (for *au contraire*)

- fate accompli (it's *fait accompli*)

- joy de vive (for *joie de vivre*)

- mon cherie (for *mon cher* or *ma chérie*)

The point is to be authentic about it. When writing in English, use French as a rare spice, and even then, only if you're sure you've used it correctly and that your audience will understand it.

It's a bête noire of mine that some people commit one faux pas after another in an attempt to project the je ne sais quoi of the crème de la crème. It may be de rigueur, but mon Dieu! I think I'll ponder this over a Montrachet at my favorite little auberge…

As Miss Piggy says, "Pretentious? Moi?"

———————————————— Mamma Mia

In the past couple of years, I've spent some time in two places where I've seen and heard Italian phrases all around me—Italy and New York City. Most of the people using Italian phrases in those places do it correctly. But what about the legions of non-Italian speakers who just want to fit in or sound suave?

Much of the trouble for Italian wannabes stems from either food or music, two of my favorite Italian exports. Oddly, when it comes to spelling Italian words and phrases, many Americans confuse them with French. Why anyone would turn to French for spelling guidance is beyond me.

Here are some examples of misunderstood Italian, the correct word or phrase, and what each means:

- **Bon appetito**

  Buon appetito. Enjoy your meal. Bwon-ah-pa-TEE-to. *Bon* is French.

- **capish**

  Capisci. Ka-PEESH-e? Understand?

- **expresso**

  Espresso. There is no x in the Italian alphabet.

- **chow, caio**

  Ciao. Goodbye or hello. Spell it right—it's only four letters.

- **Bon journo**

  Buongiorno. Good day. Bwon-JYOR-no. *Bon jour* is French.

- **Bravo, bravissimo** (for a female singer)

  Brava, bravissima. The soprano might not care as long as you're not coughing, rattling candy wrappers, answering your cell phone, wearing plaid Bermuda shorts and a fanny pack, eating popcorn, or taking flash photographs. But the people around you (your date?) will know.

I highly recommend learning to pronounce a few Italian words correctly, if only to avoid embarrassment in restaurants. Especially if you want to order something other than pizza. And imagine how many people you can impress by knowing the brava thing—even if you never actually attend an opera.

Here's another valuable Italian tip. If you find yourself in Rome and you want to communicate with the locals, just remember this: You could add an "o" to the ends of your English words and speak them with a musical lilt and a lot of arm-waving.

Italians are lovely, friendly people. They will probably smile or even laugh. But it doesn't mean they understand you.

——————————— Chasin' French

English communication is full of words and phrases that originated in French. Some survived relatively intact— *mousse, attaché,* and *carte blanche,* for example. Meanings and spellings are unchanged, and most people pronounce them more or less correctly.

But a few French expressions have morphed into something comically unrecognizable, leaving the average person with a dilemma. Do I use the words at all, and if so, how do I pronounce them?

It doesn't help that some words stopped in Britain along the way and were brutally anglicized before arriving in the USA. Brits are firm in their resolve to pronounce valet to rhyme with ballot and filet to rhyme with skillet. But they have their own history with France and I'm staying out of it.

So the well-intentioned American must choose. Do you want people to think you're a snob (a capital crime in some parts of the country) or a hick (social ostracism in others)? Here are some suggestions for avoiding embarrassment.

- **Envelope**—*AHN-vuh-lope* or *EN-vuh-lope?* Although the first is closer to the French pronunciation, you won't embarrass yourself with either pronunciation.

- **En route**—*ahn-ROOT* or *in-ROUT?* The first is closer to French and the second sounds like a conscious attempt to distance yourself from them furriners... and proud of it, dagnabbit! You can't go wrong with the first.

Ah, and here's a threesome (I want points for not making a ménage à trois joke).

1. **Chaise longue**—Original French, simply means long chair. Pronounced *shezz-lohng.*

2. **Chaise lounge**—Americans, observing that it was something used for lounging, assumed that *longue* was French for *lounge* and apparently thought they were translating it. Pronounced *shezz-lounj* or *shayz-lounj.*

3. **Chase lounge**—Metamorphosis complete. Great. Now neither word has anything to do with the original French. Chase is just a misspelling of the French word for chair and has no connection with anything. Pronounced *chase-lounj.*

Option #1, although correct, might get you accused of uppitiness. But Option #3, regrettably, suggests a lack of polish. To be safe, follow the lead of thousands of furniture dealers across the country and choose Option #2.

Just remember—it has nothing to do with chasing. Although, if you are tired from chasing someone, or something, you can always lounge on it afterward.

And, if it makes you feel better, you could call it an après-chase-chaise.

————— Two Kudos, One Kudo?

As if English weren't baffling enough, we've imported words from many other languages. And sometimes the process of assimilation grinds them up into barely recognizable bits. All the native rules for forming plurals, for example, become murky or simply go away.

Among other indignities, we subject these adopted words to back-formation. Singular Greek words, particularly those ending in s or x, sound to many English-speakers like plurals. So we feel compelled to invent a singular form that was never necessary in the original language.

Case in point—*Kudos,* a singular Greek word, originally meant congratulation or honor. Then it became popular in business (Kudos to the Quality Team for their good work) and we ended up with "…and a special kudo to the Team Leader." [Insert palm-to-forehead gesture here.]

I once attended a technical writing seminar led by a highly touted PhD expert. When an audience member asked how to deal with an off-topic piece of information, Mr. Expert said:

"Well, you could put it in an appendisee." (phonetic spelling).

It's as if, in an attempt to show off his knowledge of Greek plurals (appendices) he forgot that appendix was already a perfectly good singular word. Two kudos, one kudo. One appendix, two appendices... back-formed to one *appendice?* Does that mean we would also say one vertice, one matrice, one indice?

If we're determined to claim these words in English, it makes more sense to accept them as singular and then pluralize them in English: vertexes, matrixes, and indexes. Maybe we would be less likely to back-form them into absurd singular-sounding words. Most authoritative sources accept *appendixes* as an acceptable plural of *appendix*. My college roommate used to say (jokingly), "I have a sniffle—better get some Kleenices."

Several English words are always plural (eyeglasses, tongs, scissors, trousers, pliers), and no singular form makes sense. We often preface them with *pair of* just to be clear. Although one eyeglass could be a monocle, the others are not logically divisible. If you're into Zen, please don't write to me about the sound of one hand clapping.

Is one bit of confusion a chao? Can one person be a smartypant? Do you put one molasse on your pancakes? Bid someone an adio? Meet someone for a rendezvou? Track an undiscovered specie on a remote island... say, a Galapago?

There Is No Trophy
———————————— in Catastrophe

There must be a full moon... two occurrences of *catastrophe* misspelled in a single week. One in a newspaper, the other in a TV news graphic. And the culprits were both people who write for pay.

Catastrophe is of Greek origin and, like many words that came to us through Latin and Greek, its spelling seems strange. In most English words of more than one syllable, a final *e* is silent.

But it's in the dictionary and spell checkers know about it, so there is no excuse for writing:

catastrophy

English teachers sometimes provide students with tricks to help them remember spellings. In elementary school we were taught "I before E except after C, or if sounded as A as in neighbor and weigh." (The student who asked about *seize* was quickly shushed...)

My fourth grade teacher taught us to spell Geography with the sentence, George Eats Old Gray Rats And Paints Houses Yellow. All the little girls realized that one actually works... after we stopped squealing Eeeeeeew!

Our high school chemistry teacher told us we could remember the order of colors in the spectrum with the name Roy G. Biv (for red, orange, yellow, green, blue, indigo, violet). But we'd never heard of anyone named Biv so it was easier to memorize the color spectrum than to remember the silly name.

People's minds work in different ways. Tricks like these help some people recall rules and lessons. For others, the trick just complicates the process. It creates such a vivid mental picture that the student isn't sure if that picture is the right way or the wrong way. So it's with great caution that I warn you—the word *catastrophe* does not contain the word *trophy*.

If your fingers carelessly type *catastrophy*, picture it like this:

Unless you're writing about a feline Best in Show award, it's wrong.

Greek and Latin words can be challenging, but there is no calliopy in the merry-go-round and exaggeration is not called hyperboly. So just remember that to spell catastrophe ending in y is the epitomy of sloppy writing and a recipy for disaster.

Lost in Translation

Many Americans speak only English. As business becomes increasingly diverse and global, that embarrassing fact grows more obvious. While making fun of immigrants' accents (incidentally, how good is your Mandarin—or Arabic—or Hindi?), some people arrogantly assume that translation is easy. We don't do it, of course, because we have online tools and they do it for us.

Or do they?

Just type a phrase into the box, select the language, and... Voila! You can instantly communicate with people in their native tongue. But how do you know they're not politely suppressing a guffaw at what you said? You don't.

The epitome of dictionary-aided literal translation was captured, like a bug in amber, more than a hundred years ago by Peter Carolino in *English As She Is Spoke*. This little gem was supposed to be a Portuguese-English phrase book, but Carolino did not speak English. No problema! Using a French-English dictionary, he carefully "translated" the phrases he stole from a Portuguese-French phrase book. This exercise yielded such useful English expressions as:

- At what clock dine him?

- I am catched cold.

- I have put my stockings outward.

About four years ago, an online advertisement heralded the opening of a new shop in an upscale California mall. The Italian designer (rhymes with nada) announced:

> "The store will sell the conform residence's ready-to-wear as well as the disdainful little products for both group as well as women. The entrances have been framed by the radiant, polycarbonate curtain. The delicate, immature board lines the walls. The women's area contains seat lonesome by ivory tanned hide as well as hazed mirrors. The furnishings for the men's area underline rosewood as well as discriminating steel."

I visited the store, but did not find any disdainful little products, unless you count the sales people. The seat did not seem especially lonesome, and I didn't observe any acts of discrimination by the steel—but to be fair—I was distracted by the hazed mirrors.

English-speakers find humor in the badly translated efforts of others. But how often do we consider how our "translated" text is perceived in other languages? If, by definition,

English-only speakers don't understand the target language, we can't know how bad the translation is.

Some companies try to cut costs by machine-translating their product information. But then they don't spring for the extra bucks it takes to have it edited by a native speaker. Rather than selling their products, they only provide international customers with a good laugh.

The lesson? If you speak nothing but English, good translation requires at least one other person. Someone fluent in the other language involved. A dictionary or a software product might be helpful, but it takes a human to protect you from making a fool of yourself.

Ads—Do Not Try
This at Home

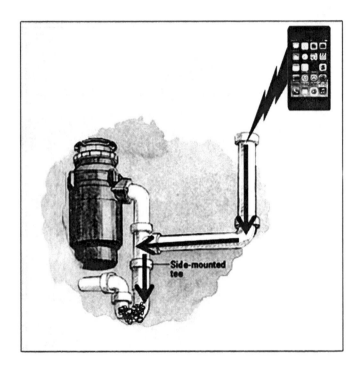

The he Internet is full of memes that illustrate how advertising can go horribly wrong. Misspelled words, double meanings, bad translations, and unfortunate pictures. And who among us has not changed the radio station when a particularly annoying commercial comes on?

Expensive national commercials talk down to their audiences:

It ain't rocket science, it ain't physics, it's just pizza.

In other words, buy my pizza cuz I'm dumb
like you.

A few American companies have learned, the hard way, that
their product names and slogans don't always translate well
for global distribution. Several failed to survive the process.
Among the best known are:

> *Come alive with the Pepsi Generation!* became *Pepsi
> will bring your ancestors back from the dead.*

> And Chevy's *Nova* in some countries meant
> *Does not go.* Wonder why it didn't sell?

But my favorites are the home-grown ads created by small,
local businesses and political candidates. There's an innocent
lack-of-awareness factor that makes them sort of charming.
Not necessarily effective, but charming.

So, no, big advertising agencies don't always get it right. But
if you try it, you'll find it's harder than it looks.

——————————— Do-it-Yourself Ads

I suppose I shouldn't assume that small businesses who do their own radio spots are always to blame for the odd—and often funny—gaffes I hear in their commercials. It's possible that a good agency would know better, but then again, not all agencies are good.

Some of the work I suspect of being homegrown is like those optical illusion graphics that look like one thing if you already know what it is, but look like something completely different if you don't.

The point is, a radio commercial should not make you unravel what the sponsor means. If you don't catch it on the first bounce, someone has wasted a lot of money.

One of the characteristics of English is that we like the objects of our verbs and prepositions to be close to them. The farther away the object is from the verb or preposition, the greater the chance that some incidental noun along the way will be perceived as the object.

Here are some examples:

Throw the cow over the fence some hay.

Toss your grandfather down the stairs his jacket.

When are you going to get out of my house the lawn chairs?

One of the easiest ways to tell that a writer is not a native English-speaker is that the word order is just a little off. But even native English speakers are subject to the problem of garbled word order. Today I heard a radio ad that said:

Why can't a plumber tell me how much it will cost to unplug my drain over the phone?

My first thoughts were, "You can unplug a drain over the phone? That's amazing! How do they do it? Sonic waves? Robots? I have to see this." The sentence should have been:

Why can't a plumber tell me over the phone how much it will cost to unplug my drain?

Another characteristic of English is that when we use multiple subjects or verbs with multiple objects, it is assumed that all actions apply to all objects. Here's another ad I've heard many times:

We will kill, eradicate, and replace all termites, rats, and old attic insulation.

I don't mind if they try to kill the attic insulation, but—really—do they have to replace the rats and termites? Can I decline that option?

Perhaps my favorite example of this multiple subject–multiple object confusion is the TV ad on behalf of some class-action law outfit:

> If you or a member of your family have suffered injury, paralysis, amputation, or death, please call this number today... 1-800-2SLEAZY.

The two uses of the word *or* mean that all subjects apply to all objects. So—stay with me here—if you, one of the subjects, have suffered death, one of the consequences, how are you hearing this commercial?

And even more important, how do you intend to pay us?

Artisans Being Artisanal

I'm not sure when it happened, but a few years ago a new bandwagon came through town and everyone jumped on it. Organic food was in, handmade was deemed better than mass-produced, and terms like *natural* and *handmade* became marketing buzzwords.

The current use of *artisan* and *artisanal* in advertising was a natural result of this trend, but few could have predicted the heights of idiocy it would reach.

Those words, meaning handmade or produced individually by some artistic process, originally suggested a superior alternative to factory-made goods. Now they're applied to items that have always been created by hand. In fact, it's hard to imagine producing them any other way. A restaurant in San Francisco announces artisanal toast. That's right, the bread is sliced by hand, some kind of spread is applied by hand, and it is placed in a toasting device... all by hand! Hard to believe, I know. Obviously it has to taste better than ordinary toast, made in a factory, the kind we all grew up on.

A national fast-food chain, known for its thirty-minute delivery guarantee, advertises artisan pizza. If it's so painstakingly
hand-crafted, I wonder if they still guarantee it will reach
you in half an hour. Do the guys make it in the car, on the
way to your house? And what's that other stuff they've been
delivering to us all these years?

An upscale bar advertises artisanal cocktails, mixed while
you watch and garnished with fruits and vegetables organ-
ically grown and sliced by hand. Thank goodness we don't
have to get our martinis and margaritas out of that impersonal vending machine anymore.

For a dry, funny take on the overuse of artisan and artisanal,
check out a book called *How to Sharpen Pencils,* by David Rees.
Everything you ever wanted to know—and more—about the
art of sharpening pencils by hand. Mr. Rees will even arti-
sanally sharpen a pencil and send it back to you for a hefty
price. But you must expect to pay for such quality and crafts-
manship, right?

And that brings me to advertising. I see lots of ads created by
people who have no idea what *artisanal*—let alone words like
bespoke, charcuterie, or *luthier*—mean. In order to understand
whether your product is truly artisanal, do a little research
before throwing the word around in an expensive ad. Are
you offering a true alternative to something mass-produced?
Maybe other words would describe your product or service
better and more accurately.

Savvy customers recognize hype when they see it nowadays,
especially since everyone claims to be an artisan and every
product is a work of art. So are you selling something that's

better than its factory-made counterparts with consistent processes, measured tolerances, and mass-production economy? I want a car that was made in a factory.

At least, if you choose to use the words *artisan* or *artisanal*, get it right. Today I saw a magazine ad for a hairstylist who describes herself as a Manhattan Hair *Artesian*. For the uninitiated, *artesian* describes a water source that causes water to spring from the ground under positive pressure. A large, expensive ad (sixteen hundred dollars per placement—I looked it up), and she's going to give you a hairdo that looks like a natural spring? Water spouting out the top of your head? Or is water spouting out the top of *her* head? Either way...

Thank goodness it's not one of those hairstyles that rolls off the assembly line just like everyone else's. And, unlike other stylists, she's going to style your hair by hand. The styling is probably expensive, but she, not some robotic arm, is actually going to hold the shears and the blow dryer.

You can expect to pay more for this service because, misspelled or not, someone has to pay for those *artesianal* ads.

Telltale Signs

The Internet should have taught us to say a lot in a small space. Website real estate is valuable. Twitter, as well as most entry fields, has a character limit. Online headings need to be eye-catching, succinct, and unambiguous. But these lessons appear lost on the people who make signs.

I'm not talking about hand-lettered signs by the roadside announcing *cantelopes* and *avacado's*. Or signs with typos or embarrassing non-English mistakes. I mean expensive metal signs, paid for by businesses, public agencies, and state highway departments. Not technically ungrammatical, but subject to more than one interpretation.

The principles are the same for signs and written headlines. The most common problems are words that function as different parts of speech, missing punctuation, unclear antecedents, passive verbs, and misplaced modifiers. Some signs cry out for a response—another sign below or beside the original. Here are my favorites, followed by the accompanying signs I'd like to see:

- **Wash & Vacuum Senior Citizens $15.95**

  But You Can Wash & Vacuum a Teenager for $10

- **Caution Pedestrians Slippery When Wet**

  Easier to Catch Them When They're Dry

- **Shirts and Shoes Must be Worn**

  But Your Pants Can be Brand New

- **This Door is Alarmed**

  Other Door Just Mildly Concerned

- **Prepare to Stop When Flashing**

  At Least Button Trench Coat

Before creating a sign or a headline, weigh each word carefully. Ask yourself if there is any possible way the message could be misinterpreted. Is there a passive verb? A double entendre lurking somewhere? An implied pronoun? One of those words that is sometimes a noun and sometimes a verb or adjective?

Communicating with just a few words is harder than it looks. Collections of funny signs and headlines routinely circulate on the Internet and show up in mass mailings. But some are not intrinsically funny, they just cause readers to scratch their heads in wonder.

So I suggest this:

**Stop
Confusing
Signs**

They're bewildered enough already.

Too Much Information

Some time ago, the American viewing public surrendered its sense of shame. Reality TV made overnight stars of people with no discernible talent, but a willingness to make idiots of themselves on national television. Networks pandered to the lowest common denominator, and audiences tuned in for their daily dose of embarrassment, revulsion, and disgust.

People competed for prize money by lying in coffins with thousands of cockroaches. Some guy traveled the world, eating monkey brains and live worms. Prime-time sitcoms joked about bodily functions and vomiting. It became more and more difficult to shock people or even to get their attention. So in order to sell products, advertisements changed along with the public's tolerance for vulgarity.

Thanks to this mass desensitization, I know far too much about medical conditions I don't have, and why other people need treatment for them. Ads are graphic and specific. You'd think the target audience, people with intimate or distasteful conditions, would be well aware of their unpleasant symptoms.

A commercial for a dental clinic sends me grasping for the car radio's OFF button every time I hear the opening line: *Do you have rotting teeth, bleeding gums, and bad breath?* Then there are the TV ads. Is there no better way to sell condoms, feminine hygiene products, bathroom tissue, and cures for everything from skin rashes to erectile dysfunction? Do we need to be told what those products are for and how to use them? That's what package inserts are for.

Ever since icky went mainstream, I've noticed a lack of manners and decorum, even in business and social communications. Etiquette is not knowing which fork to use, it's consideration for other people's feelings. So if your writing or speech makes other people nauseated or uncomfortable, to be shocking, attention-getting, or just clueless, it's impolite. More important, unless your audience consists of nineteen-year-old frat boys, it can derail the purpose of your communication.

For an audience of medical professionals or disease-sufferers, of course you have to be descriptive and clinical. But I'm talking about general audiences and respecting the boundaries of appropriateness. I once received one of those chatty Christmas letters in which a woman wrote a full page describing the gory—I'm not kidding—details of her husband's abdominal surgery. It actually contained this phrase: The green drainage has finally stopped.

Let's just agree that the desired response to your holiday greeting probably isn't *Eeeeeeeew!*

What ever happened to just the right amount of information? At the opposite end of the information spectrum, a few TV ads provide none at all. Remember the perfume ad with a handsome but scruffy Hollywood leading man who mumbled, "It's not a journey... every journey ends but we go on... wherever I go, there you are... inevitable..."?

I wonder if they would have sold more perfume if he'd just said, "Look, this stuff smells nice. I look like a vagrant, but I clean up good. If you wore this perfume I would like you."

—————— Three Times Less Sensible

You've heard them, I'm sure. Shouting from radio, TV, and the Internet—ads that promise x times less of something. Here are some of my favorite examples:

- This paper towel is so strong you can use four times less!

- This spray cleaner leaves five times less residue!

- A home with a security system is three times less likely to have a break-in than a home without one!

These examples demonstrate errors in forming arithmetic comparisons. They assume that *times less* is an inverted form of *times as much*. In fact, they are not direct opposites at all.

A times-as-much comparison of two quantities requires a base (basis of comparison) and a multiplier. Even if you don't specify the base, it's just a matter of multiplying one number by another. Our paper towel does the job with one sheet, another brand requires four. Ours takes two, theirs takes eight. Simple.

But in a less-than comparison, you need an exact number or a multiplier expressed as a percent, a fraction, or a decimal. Let's say a competing brand of paper towel takes four sheets to absorb a spill. If you claim your brand requires four times less, what does that even mean?

¼ as many sheets (one)?

25% less (three)?

0.25 less (three)?

something else?

It's simple arithmetic. If the times-less number is one or greater and you multiply it by the base (the times part) and then subtract that number from the Base (the less-than part), the result is either zero or a negative number. To say it requires four times less literally means this:

4 (the base)

− 16 (four times the base)

− 12

You get twelve paper towels back?

Sometimes the advertiser doesn't want you to know the exact numbers. Suppose your home has a three-percent likelihood of being burglarized and a security system would reduce that to one percent. If you knew that, you might decide that three percent isn't such a scary statistic and you'll take your chances. Three times less likely (than what?) means nothing, but it sounds impressive. Especially if you're scared into imagining that your danger is much greater.

So how would you handle this headache-inducing dilemma? If you're determined to avoid actual numbers, just turn it around.

- This paper towel is so absorbent, other brands require four times as much!

- Other spray cleaners leave five times as much residue as our brand!

- A home without a security system is three times more likely to have a break-in than a home with one!

The product you're selling is now the base. You're not revealing it, but it is a definable number. And if you did reveal it, the concept of times-as-much would make sense.

But here's the best solution:

Use Brand X spray cleaner and inferior paper towels to clean your windows. The residue buildup on the glass prevents anyone from seeing through it. Assuming that people with streaky windows probably don't have anything worth stealing, burglars will move on down the street to another house.

Voila! Security system.

——————— Write Like You Mean It

L *ike you mean it*. This trendy expression has popped up in advertising and social media like a plague of mushrooms. Purists—let's forget for a minute that many would correct it to *as if you mean it*. The worst thing about it is the implication. If you don't do what the ad tells you, you're a slacker.

So how can you make sure to do everything like you mean it?

Eat like you mean it

Stuff an obscene amount of meat, bread, cheese, and drippy sauce into your mouth all at once. Anything else is phoning it in. A reasonable amount of food you can eat like a civilized person is—well—eating like you don't mean it. By the way, that skinny model is just pretending to mean it.

Vacation like you mean it

Take your family to an expensive theme park instead of going camping. For the same amount of money you could take them all to Europe... but then your children would grow up emotionally scarred. Picture them years later in handcuffs, being interviewed on Dateline. "My parents took me to London, Paris, and Firenze, but they didn't mean it."

Shop like you mean it

Go to the biggest mall you can find and load yourself down with bags of designer clothing and shoes. Put it all on your maxed-out credit cards and worry about it tomorrow. And for Pete's sake, don't patronize small, local businesses where no one will see you carrying those high-end shopping bags. No exposure there. What's the point?

If doing everything with total commitment and gusto is such a good thing, there should be signs in gyms that say *Exercise like you mean it*. How about libraries? *Read like you mean it*. And this one should come with every personal computer:

Write like you mean it

Re-read and correct. Spell-check. Look things up. Verify facts. Cut excessive modifiers and prepositions. Use active verbs. Avoid clichés, jargon, and buzzwords. Use an editor.

Much of what we read online and in periodicals is so poorly written it's shocking. Misspelled words, typos, factual errors, unsupported opinions. Not just the crazies who comment and rant, but the sources we rely on for news. Public figures and professionals seem to have forgotten how to write.

In a social climate of rampant intolerance, all factions seem to agree on one thing. If you publish mistakes, or even lies, and someone catches them, you can always say... "I didn't mean it."

—————— Hyperbole out of Control

Everyone exaggerates a little now and then. Advertisers have to do it in order to sell products. But in elevating their claims to outshine the competition, ad writers have reached a tipping point.

In an unspoken agreement between advertisers and consumers, we all expect outrageous statements. We don't believe most of them, and we're not expected to. Many are done for comedic effect. A radio spokesman for a mortgage company shouts that choosing their low-cost financing is...

... the biggest no-brainer in the history of mankind!

I always imagine one caveman saying to another, "Fire. Hot. Hurt." There must be other examples of bigger no-brainers (Woolly Mammoth! Run!), although much of mankind's history was not recorded so there's no proof.

A frozen panini package gives directions for cooking the contents in the microwave, using the...

... revolutionary browning tray!

It's the box, folks. You turn the box inside-out and place the sandwich on top of it. Revolutionary? Hardly comparable to that little unpleasantness with England in 1776. Or the French unrest in 1789. Or that 1917 dust-up in Russia.

So we take these claims with a grain of salt. Or do we? Perhaps we're so conditioned to expect exaggeration that the line between truth and hyperbole has moved. The question is... in which direction?

A medical web site recently published an article that encouraged people with desk jobs to get up and move around periodically. It listed the dangers of working for hours while hunched over a computer, and identified some health problems that could result. Someone misinterpreted the article and published this bold statement:

> Every minute you sit at your desk takes years
> off your life!

The claim was picked up and quoted, unquestioned, in dozens of other articles and blogs. The original article was well-intentioned, but stop and think about that misquoted sentence. If every minute you sat still in a chair took even one year off your life, most people would have died long before they were born. That includes anyone who has ever...

- Attended a concert

- Driven a hundred miles in a car

- Seen a movie in a theater

- Waited in a doctor's office

- Watched a football game on TV

- Flown across the country in an airplane

Maybe it's time to apply a correction factor to everything we read and hear. I once knew an honest-to-goodness drama queen who spoke almost entirely in exaggerations. Everything was more unbelievable, over the top, and simply amazing than whatever anyone else had ever seen.

Her family followed her around like a Truth Squad, explaining, "Take everything she says and divide it by ten."

Slogans That Went Astray

O h, to be a fly on the wall when commercial and political slogans are being composed. I'd love to know the reasoning behind the decisions that give us ungrammatical or ill-advised catchphrases.

In some cases the perpetrators must have made a conscious decision to talk down to their demographic. That's not very flattering. In other cases, it seems more likely that they just didn't know any better.

Consider these examples:

A third less calories than regular beer…

The difference between *fewer* and *less* is a subject for another discussion. Let's just say here that it should be either *fewer calories* or *less fattening*, but not *less calories*. Perhaps the beer folks feared their target market (Bubba?) would not understand that.

This one is from a restaurant chain:

Live adventurous.

Aside from the fact that it's just a verb and an adjective (that should be an adverb, *adventurously*), what does it say about a restaurant if eating there constitutes an adventure? Is it the adrenalin rush you get from wondering if you'll get food poisoning?

Famous maker of electronic gadgets advises:

Think different.

Again, the adjective should be an adverb (*differently*), if that's even what they mean. With a little punctuation, it could imply *Think—Innovative!* or *Think, "Fabulous!"* But there is no punctuation and that's a little obscure for a two-word slogan anyway. Deliberately using an ungrammatical slogan is, in effect, condescending to your target market, assuming they won't notice or care, and thumbing your nose at anyone who does.

My all-time favorites are political slogans. Some seem to be just begging for parody or derision. A recent local campaign for a mature woman seeking re-election was not ungrammatical, but it was ill-advised. She distributed canvas tote bags with this slogan printed on them: *Re-use, Recycle, Re-elect.* Am I the only one who, as a woman over forty, would rather not be identified with the idea of a reusable bag?

The funniest one of all was a political ad that aired in Seattle for a candidate seeking to emphasize her humble roots:

Her father poured concrete, her mother a secretary...

As editors and writers often do, I emailed this to my co-worker and legendary editor, Phil. I said, "Her mother poured a secretary?" Always quick on the draw, Legendary Phil responded within seconds:

... a martini, and her heart out.

Anthropomorphize This

A
nthropomorphism. An almost unpronounceable word... giving human characteristics to something that isn't human. It has a long tradition in mythology and fiction, as we associate human traits—even genders and names—with hurricanes, star formations, and sailing vessels. It's not altogether a bad thing. Without it, there would be fewer fairy tales and Disney movies. It even makes sense for an animated bear to tell children they shouldn't start forest fires.

But many advertisers think anthropomorphizing is cute, and cute sells. So they make some very odd things into little characters with faces and voices, and you have to wonder what message they're trying to communicate.

- A pest control service portrays termites as lovable little characters with Alvin-and-the-Chipmunks voices. Termites are not lovable. The object is to kill them before they eat your house.

- Another pest control service shows a man holding a giant hammer behind his back, staring at an adorable little mouse with a quizzical look on his face. Mice and rats are vermin, and you don't want them in your house. If they're cute, do you still want to kill them?

- A brand of chicken portrays two scruffy characters as wannabe poultry candidates their company would never accept. They lie about being all natural, hormone-free, and so on. Think about this. They're not trying to get into Stanford. They're trying to be accepted by a chicken processing plant where they will be killed and eaten. Who does that, even in cartoons?

Humanizing in commercials is not always bad, but it seems counter-productive if the point is to eat or eradicate the humanized character.

Anthropomorphism also creeps into technical and business writing. Especially those books with titles like *Quantum Physics Made Ridiculously Easy for Complete Idiots*. Some things just shouldn't be trivialized, humanized, or animated. And trying to make them fun (1) usually fails, and (2) does nothing to make the subject easier to understand.

- If the system thinks the printer is not installed, it will give you an error message.

- Other applications might be interested in the information you've stored in your database.

- The barium sulfate particles resulting from the reaction want to fall to the bottom of the tube.

- Processors of that type don't understand FORTRAN syntax.

Computer systems and chemicals don't think, express interest, want to fall, or understand. They detect, access, precipitate, and interpret. If you're tempted to humanize the subjects of your writing, ask yourself if it will enhance your message or confuse the reader.

My favorite quotation on this subject is from Michael Ernst, a professor of Computer Science and Engineering at the University of Washington:

"Don't anthropomorphize computers. They hate it."

Chagrin and Other
———— Misfortunes

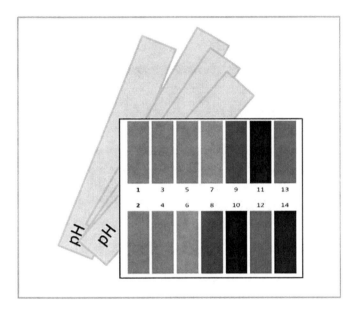

Are we judged by the words we use? Absolutely.

Like it or not, your audience gets to have an opinion about you whenever you write or speak. That means every time you utter a sentence. To anyone. A dear friend, your boss, an auditorium full of people, an entire TV viewership, a doorman, or a cashier at the grocery store. Although sometimes it matters to you what they think, often you just don't care. Do you tailor your speech to the situation, or are you the same person to everyone you meet?

In rare cases, you might actually be pleased if your audience disapproves of you. For example, many ignorant people are dismissive—even mocking—when faced with something they don't understand. It's a defense mechanism. They reject a word or an idea rather than admit they don't understand or appreciate it. The idea is to make you feel belittled or dismissed and deflect attention away from their own ignorance. Recognize this behavior for what it is, and judge for yourself whether to succumb to the temptation to fit in.

Hey there cutie, wanna dance?

Thank you, but no.

Aw, c'mon! Whatsa matter—you lame or somethin'?

No, just a little fatigued.

Fah-TEEGED! Well LAH-DEE-DAH! Ain't you some kinda stuck-up [expletive deleted]!

This is where you get to decide whether that opinion matters to you.

The Litmus List

I was once admonished by a sleazy guy at a party for using the word *chagrin*. He recoiled as if I were a snake, saying, "Honey, if you ever want to catch a man you'll stop using words like that."

When I recovered from the shock—that he thought I was trying to catch him, as opposed to tolerating his painful small talk—it occurred to me that the word *chagrin* could serve as a useful conversational litmus test. So I resolved to use it as often as possible, to weed out men like him. And, by the way, I don't mean purely socially. The litmus list is subconsciously at work even if I'm interviewing a client or a job candidate.

Many people of both genders have their own pronunciation litmus tests, whether they realize it or not. It's a collection of words that, when mispronounced, or spelled the way they are mispronounced, cause the user to drop several points in the listener's opinion. The offender might be physically attractive, charming, or successful, but there's always that nagging mistake. Regional American accents notwithstanding, modern communications leave no excuse for these:

- **asterick**—There is a risk in asterisk.

- **expresso**—Good espresso may not be fast. No x.

- **mischievious**—Mischievous has three syllables. MISS-chu-vuss, not miss-CHEE-vee-uss.

- **nucular**—Nuclear. Even educated Texans say NEW-cle-ur.

- **sherbert**—Sherbet does not rhyme with Herbert. Only one r. SHUR-bet.

- **taunt**—If you mean taut, tight, as in stretched, it rhymes with *fought*, not *want*.

This bonus word has caught on, especially in tech circles in recent years, but that doesn't make it correct:

- **processeez**—Processes. It's PRAH-cess-uz. Brits and Canadians get a pass on PROE-cess-uz, but the plural of process is not PRAH-cess-EEZ.

It registers as a bungled affectation. People must hear index-indices, analysis-analyses, and like the way it sounds. But those words are of Greek origin and that is how plurals are formed for those words. *Process* is not a Greek word. Neither is *princess*. Or *abscess*.

So if the Man of My Dreams ever saunters up at a conference and asks, "Where is the session on Business ProcessEEZ?"... well, you can imagine my chagrin.

Writing It Down

S poken idioms and expressions are often wrong. Popular examples include *I could care less, for all intensive purposes,* and *take it for granite.* In most cases, the speaker is just being careless.

Speech evaporates as soon as the words are spoken, understood, and replaced with more speech. But the act of writing it down imposes additional requirements.

You're now held accountable for proper spelling and, most of all, sense. Readers can read it again. They can copy it and share it with others. If it doesn't make sense, they might even have a good laugh.

In the olden days, when published works guaranteed at least some minimum level of editing, silly errors were rare. Books, magazines, and newspapers used professional writers and editors. We learned to write well by reading well-written material. But with the advent of Internet news sources and e-zines, young readers have a virtual landfill of bad writing at their—um—disposal.

Here are three recent examples from "professionally" written online articles:

- Hard to believe in this stay and age...

  The writer means *in this day and age*, and it's possible that someone could misunderstand that if it were spoken. But do people even read what they write? It makes no sense at all.

- It's good to exercise regularly, but don't overdue it...

  Exercise is something you shouldn't *overdo*, but *overdue* is more suited to bills and library books. You see, children, once upon a time they had buildings full of actual books you could borrow, and you were supposed to return them by a certain... oh, never mind.

- We expected a live performance, but all she did was lip-sing...

  Allowing for the fact that it's hard to sing without using your lips, this writer meant the performer only pretended to sing by synchronizing her lip movements with a recording. Spelled *lip-synch* or *lip-sync*, but not lip-sing.

Technology now allows us to publish our thoughts instantly. Without verification, editing, or even review. Autocorrect steps in and changes words we don't want changed. Our fingers hit neighboring keys and we make embarrassing typos.

The least we can do is try to produce the best first effort, and then review. Double-check. Look things up.

It's great when a piece of writing goes viral and thousands of readers see it. Not so great when your name is forever associated with a blunder.

Just ask Bill Buckner (1986 World Series, Game Six).

Do We Need
—————————— Grammar Police?

People who correct others' English grammar and usage mistakes... are they grammar police? I guess it depends on how they do it.

As with any other embarrassing attribute (bad table manners, crude language, body odor), bad grammar is least likely to be important to those who have it. And there is almost no polite way to point it out.

In most cases, if you call attention to a mistake, the culprit is defensive, thinks you're pedantic, or worse, and discounts your criticism. *Who cares? It's not important. You know what I meant.* Unless they ask for correction, it's probably better to let it go.

Criticism stings, even (or especially), for people who pride themselves on their careful use of English. They're the ones who do care, and they don't expect to be corrected.

So how important is it to use precise, correct language? If your circle of acquaintances is very small and you have few interactions with other people, maybe not at all. But if you travel, work in a large company, deal with the public, or write for publication, your audience is bound to include non-native English speakers. They often learn English the way it is supposed to be, not the way we use it when we're being lazy. And we all get lazy. Yes, all of us.

Here are two sentences, both from published articles. The writers leave it to you to figure out what they mean. A diligent English student, parsing these sentences by the book, would be confused.

1. These casseroles are just as good now as they were as a kid.

    The casseroles used to be children, and now they are adults?

    Better—These casseroles are just as good now as they were when you were a kid.

2. By downloading this white paper the sponsor may contact you.

    When the sponsors download the white paper, they have permission to contact me?

    Better—By downloading this white paper, you agree to let the sponsor contact you.

Even the self-confessed grammar police can experience a comeuppance. Last summer in Indonesia, I met a visiting family with two small sons. The mother is German. The

French father works for an Italian company. Son Victor (age seven) speaks German, French, English, and a little Italian.

A local family was trying to train a dog, Dogé, not to jump up on people. When he planted his muddy paws on the knees of my beige slacks, I said, "Dogé—you can't jump on people!"

Seven-year-old Victor politely observed, in his third—yes, third—language:

"Really, he *can*. We just don't want him to do it."

Ouch.

You Know You're a
————————— Geezer When...

First, geezerness can occur at any age. You don't have to be old to be a geezer. Simply be gullible, disregard anything current, and resist change. Get stuck in a decade and refuse to move out of it. That decade could be the nineties or the two-thousands, so don't think that youth disqualifies you.

Even if you've never met them, you can spot geezers by the way they communicate.

There must be a basement somewhere full of moldy short-hand and typing books from the fifties. In those days, high school girls were taught how to write proper business letters. Boys took wood shop or something. After all, they would be dictating the letters. How these books escaped into the real world is a mystery, but they are still infecting communication sixty years later. You might be a geezer if you ever write:

- Dear Sir or Madam

- Please remit to me soonest

- Sending under separate cover

- With reference to your above-mentioned

- Enclosed herewith is the letter per your request of the sixth

- Very truly yours, Sincerely yours (*Yours* is an archaic contraction of *Your servant*. Are you a footman?)

Another way to tell if you're a geezer is to examine your personal email habits.

- Have you built a huge group email distribution list? Hundreds of dear friends?

- Does this list include school classmates, ex-spouses, old flames, random acquaintances, people you've never actually met, distant relatives, clients, and co-workers?

- Do you expose all of their email addresses in your messages?

- Do you subject the entire list to every HILARIOUS joke, AMAZING photograph, INSPIRING story, or UNBELIEVABLE YouTube clip you see? Do you comment in ALL-CAPS?

- Do you think all those photos and YouTube videos are for real?

- Do you actually believe those urban legends?

We all send links and jokes to selected friends from time to time, so please don't think I'm picking on old people. At least they don't write, "C U @ mall b4 2 cuz I havnt 8." Just remember that, if your email habits are like those listed above, you might need to wise up or get a hobby.

Keep other people's email addresses private. It's not difficult, and it's just common courtesy. You know all of your friends, but they don't know each other and don't want to. I hate to burst any bubbles, but many—or most—of those soupy books of inspirational true stories are fiction. And if something is too amazing to be real, it's probably digitally altered or staged. In fact, there are websites that debunk the most popular AMAZING things circulating on the Web. You might want to check them out before sharing anything with your four hundred best friends.

Today I received an email from a Nigerian prince who needs my help to get a large sum of his family's money out of the country. Seemed like such a nice young man. He's offering to share his fortune with me if I will send him my bank account numbers.

What do you think I should do?

Single Man Seeking
Woman

An increasing number of couples meet online these days, and people are discovering how critical communication is in describing yourself to prospective love interests. But a code has developed, so several friends and I have decided to provide this list as a service to single women. A translation of some phrases that raise red flags.

To be fair, men were invited to participate too. Their suggestions follow in the next article.

Here's what the ladies report:

- Top-secret government job. Can't say too much about it. Security, you know.

  I'm married.

- Long walks on the beach... quiet evenings by the fire... candlelight dinners at home...

I'm cheap and I'll never take you anywhere.
And I expect you to cook.

- Reformed bad boy

My parole officer says I'm doing much better.

- Old-fashioned guy

Chauvinist. Want a compliant woman who won't give me any backtalk.

- Mature gent

RV, yellow polyester bermudas with sandals, black socks, the whole nine yards.

- Affectionate, warm, cuddly

All hands. I intend to jump your bones on our first date. Maybe before.

- Family is most important to me.

I still live at home with my mother.

- Romantic

Yeah, sure, whatever. I'll tell you anything you want to hear just to get you into bed.

- Conservative, religious, stand-up guy

Rush Limbaugh fan. Judgmental, up-tight, and fault-finding. You're probably not good enough for me anyway.

- Money is not important to me.

  I don't have any.

- I like a liberated woman...

  ... who pays for her own dinner.

- Outdoorsman, enjoy hunting and fishing

  You'll spend every weekend alone while I'm stalking animals in the woods.

- Enjoy going to movies

  As long as they have explosions, car chases, or lots of nudity.

- Big guy, athletic build

  Enormous beer belly. The only athletic activities I'm fit for are Sumo wrestling and watching football on TV.

- Free spirit. Don't care for the corporate rat-race. I am my own person. I don't bow to The Man.

  I don't have a job.

- Unpretentious, casual, laid-back kinda guy

  You'll never catch me in a suit and tie or even a sport coat. I'll wear a ratty T-shirt and flip-flops to your cousin's wedding.

- Id rly lk 2 mt u

  I'm either trying to make you think I'm young and hip or I'm hiding the fact that I can't spell. Maybe both.

Single Woman
Seeking Man

M ale readers think I'm a little tough on them when I write about what men really mean in online dating profiles. One of them said, "Is there nothing a man can say?" He's right. I should have said that men might mean something other than what their profiles indicate. Just as women might mean something different. Shocking, I know, but men don't have a monopoly on deception.

It's possible—though not likely—that people of both genders are being one hundred percent honest when they describe themselves online. It's just good to remember that presenting yourself honestly is about the hardest communication task there is.

Just in case, here's why men should be wary:

- Looking for marriage or a serious relationship.

  My company laid me off and I need a meal ticket—fast.

- I have a grown son.

  He's been sleeping on my sofa while he looks for a job. For six years.

- Earthy, natural kind of girl...

  Aging hippie—I don't wear deodorant or shave my legs.

- I'm young but I just loooove older men.

  Sugar daddies are, like, totally the best.

- I dress for comfort, no slave to fashion.

  Tent tops, white cropped pants with giant white granny panties showing through, orthopedic shoes.

- Hot chick, fun lady, life of any party.

  After a few drinks I have no inhibitions. I was really popular in high school.

- My religion is the most important thing to me.

  You'd better be prepared to give me a ring before sampling the merchandise.

- Low-maintenance, easy-going, always sunny and cheerful... no matter what.

Passive-aggressive. If you cross me, I'll smile but I'll get you back when you least expect it.

- Meat and potatoes kind of cook.

  Lots of carbs and cholesterol. Hamburger Helper, red meat, bacon, eggs, desserts. Is your life insurance paid up?

- Hilarious, edgy sense of humor.

  Snarky, sarcastic, negative. No one is safe, not even you.

- One-man woman, loyal and devoted.

  You're mine. I'll go through your pockets, stalk you, have you followed.

- High fashion. Striking. I look like a model.

  Self-absorbed. Nothing but the best for me. Be prepared to buy me expensive gifts and pretend you don't see me checking out better-looking guys everywhere we go.

- Total romantic, looking for that one magical soul mate who "gets" me.

  Read my mind, remember every important date in our relationship with appropriate gestures. Or I'll sulk and won't tell you why. You're supposed to know.

- Look much younger than my age.

  Cougar on the prowl...

- Bubbly, outgoing, cute, fun, never met a stranger.

  I chatter non-stop and you'll never get a word
  in. By the end of our first date you'll want to
  climb out the men's room window to escape.

- Will i am 22 i grew up in santa,fe texas I have to ba-
  bies... **

  I will make you feel very, very smart.

  ** I'm not being intentionally cruel. This is an
  actual post.

This was all in fun, of course. Not only do we not see ourselves
as others see us, but we also communicate it badly. The ideal
communication is probably one-way. One party does all the
talking and the other just listens.

In other words, for the most trouble-free, honest, and affectionate companionship, maybe the safest solution is... get a dog.

Just Making Conversation

If you're one of those people who never met a stranger, you're going to think I'm a real grouch. Even if you're not, you may still think I'm a grouch but that's beside the point. I think I'm a private person and that there are lots of people like me.

The super-friendly person often starts a conversation by asking a question. If I don't feel like answering, I become the bad guy. They are, after all, just making conversation and I don't want to play.

Those who deal with the public all the time (retail clerks, airline gate agents, waiters) probably get tired of making polite chit-chat with the people they see all day long. And yet their employers have apparently told them to engage the customers in conversation and show an interest in them as individuals. What's missing here is a definition of how to do that without intruding on personal privacy. Some things just need to be spelled out.

It's fine to make conversation about the weather, the traffic, how the local baseball team is doing, but some topics are potentially insulting or intrusive. Before just making conversation, it's often a good idea to count to three—slowly—and ask yourself if it's inappropriate or just none of your business.

Some questions I've been asked by complete strangers make me want to say something outrageous. Just to see if they're paying attention. To turn the question back on the questioners so they can feel embarrassed. I would never actually do that, but I think about it. These inane questions show how easy it is to misinterpret a set of items or circumstances and why you should leave them alone.

Here are some answers I wish I'd given:

- Airline ticket agent—(Glancing at some random stranger behind me in line) Soooo—are you and your husband going on a vacation?

  Shhhh! He's not my husband. We're both married to other people and our spouses think we're on a business trip.

- Fabric store clerk—What are you going to make with all this pink flannel?

  A disguise. I plan to rob a bank dressed as a giant bunny.

- Hardware store cashier—Hmm—concrete patch, padlock, rebar—what kind of project are you doing?

A modest torture chamber under my house... nothing fancy.

- Rental car agent—So what brings you here—business or pleasure?

Seriously? I'm in the middle of <bleeping> nowhere. Who would come here for pleasure?

- Business supply clerk—That'll be $25.60, with $2.11 tax (eye-roll) for the governor... bummer, right?

I voted for him.

- Gift shop clerk—Wednesday is Senior Discount Day. Shall I ring it up with the discount?

I'm 29. I've had a hard life.

The corporate offices of a grocery store in my neighborhood once required that all cashiers look at your check or credit card and then say your name three times during checkout. Some expert had told them that people like this.

"There you go, Rebecca. Thanks for shopping with us, Rebecca. See you next time, Rebecca." Three times. Just in case that creepy guy behind me in line who had followed me from the frozen food section, and is now going to follow me into the parking lot, didn't hear it the first two times.

If your occupation puts you in contact with the public, re-member that some people just want a pleasant—and anon-ymous—business transaction, not a new best pal. As for the grocery store, their policy did affect my buying behavior. I limited my purchases there to small, incidental things in cash, and shopped at another store for groceries.

The company mandate apparently doesn't have a guideline for that.

—————————— You Know—Humility

Everyone knows it's rude to make fun of people. Especially for being ignorant. Often, people who have not learned something just lack exposure and opportunity. But I once worked with a group of people who found a loophole in this rule.

The Sales and Marketing department in our small company included several wise-cracking, funny, literate salesmen. They were smart young men who enjoyed their work camaraderie and sometimes behaved like overgrown frat boys. The department also included a low-level administrative employee with abominable, often embarrassing, communication skills.

Her spelling and grammatical errors were legendary, and the sales guys often had to rewrite or cover them up when communicating with customers. On the phone with trucking companies she routinely asked for the bill of ladies (bill of lading) and she once seriously used the phrase self-defecating humor (self-deprecating humor). Yeah.

To complicate matters, this inarticulate employee had delusions of grandeur. She referred to herself as a female executive, and participated in nasty office gossip and back-stabbing at every opportunity. No one was spared. Because of her attitude, the sales guys considered her fair game. Their favorite pastime was to bait her with a word they knew she would not understand. When she asked what it meant, they would answer with a synonym they knew she would also not understand. The conversations went something like this:

The operation was completely *clandestine*.

What's that?

You know—*surreptitious*.

He was really *obsequious*.

What's that?

You know—*sycophantic*.

Her face was *inscrutable*.

What's that?

You know—*enigmatic*.

They knew that pride would prevent her from asking a second time, so they enjoyed watching her pretend to understand the answer. It wasn't nice at all, but it was an example of what happens when you act as if you know more than you do. It puts a Kick Me sign on your back. Most people learn by first admitting they don't know everything, and they look things up. They read. Listen. Pay attention. Double-check.

This is why I advocate writing within your comfort zone. It's when we step out of that area that we get into trouble. But we should always be trying to expand that comfort zone. I learn something every day, especially from fellow writers and editors. With vocabulary-building, as well as other skills, sometimes the first step to learning is a little diffidence.

You know—humility.

Write, Edit, Earn
──Dozens of Dollars

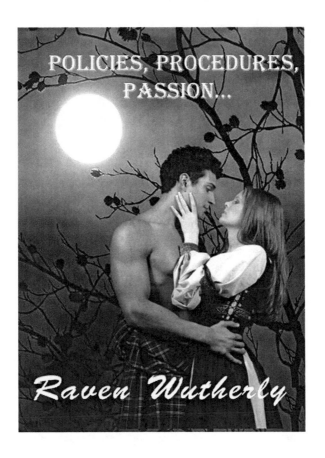

Agreat editor can make a mediocre writer look good. A
good writer, working with the same editor, can look terrific. Editors are the makeup artists and sound engineers

of the writing world. Some of your favorite actors or singers would be a crashing disappointment if you ran into them at Walmart or heard them sing the National Anthem a cappella at a ballgame. If you saw the unedited drafts of some best-selling novels, you'd be horrified. And that doesn't even include the romances.

It's a shame editors are not valued more in our society. If they were, they'd be paid better and given more credit for the success of their finished products. In order for a skill to be valued, it must be recognized. That requires evaluation by someone with half a brain who would know good editing if it bit them in the... well, you get the idea.

So why do we even bother to write well and edit our work? Because the end result is more likely to succeed and achieve its intended purpose than if we don't. The unsuspecting public might not realize why it works, because the benefits of good, well-edited writing are subtle. The public just knows that they understand it, it maintains their interest, they learn from it, it makes them laugh, or it convinces them to buy something.

Reasons enough.

Show, Don't Tell

Fiction writers have much to teach the rest of us. Your business or general communication probably doesn't require character or plot development. Still, good fiction writers know their audiences well and make their points with great skill.

The average person, in day-to-day communication, makes a strong point by telling the reader what to think. We all make the classic amateur mistakes. Most of us load up with modifiers (adjectives and adverbs), repeat the point, make it bold or all capitals, or add exclamation points at the end. Fiction writers gently lead you to the conclusions they want you to have... so that the ideas seem like yours, not theirs.

Here are some examples:

- Telling—It was night. She was quite terrified and his voice was very scary!

- Showing—The street had grown dark, and her throat was so dry she could not swallow. Footsteps. Suddenly, the sound of his voice sent a shiver down her spine.

- Telling—He was really, really, really HANDSOME.

- Showing—She stood, transfixed. Unable to tear her gaze away from his strong jaw, prominent cheekbones, and dark lashes fringing azure-blue eyes that seemed to look into her soul.

OK, so this is why I leave fiction to those who are good at it. The point is, the same technique applies to other kinds of writing. Start with the assumption that your readers have no reason to agree with you. When you make your bold statement, anticipate the question *Why?* When you show evidence, it's more effective than just expecting them to accept your point.

- Telling—It's absolutely important to do this step!

  Showing—If you skip this step, all of your data will be lost and you will have to start all over again.

- Telling—We need to adopt this policy right away!

  Showing—The law is changing in six weeks. If we do nothing, we will suffer an increased tax burden.

- Telling—You really should buy this inexpensive, economical software.

  Showing—This software will save you 20% per year in labor costs alone.

- Telling—Our office is a disgusting dump. We need to refurbish it.

  Showing—Our carpet is stained, the walls are dingy, and the lighting is so poor that clients are making negative comments about it.

You might not ever write an exciting thriller or a steamy bodice-ripper, but readers need a reason to believe you. Remember—*because I said so* is appropriate only with your children. And even then, it doesn't work.

——————————— Gender-bending

The Women's Movement gave rise to some well-intentioned but laughable language suggestions. The effort to remove gender references from job titles brought us *journeyperson, councilperson,* and *waitperson.*

When it became clear that "person" was not the answer, gender-neutral titles evolved into something more sensible. Mailman became mail carrier. Fireman became fire fighter, and so on.

But other words rode the pendulum-swing into silliness (<u>her</u>story instead of <u>his</u>tory?). And, every few years, someone comes up with a way to keep us from having to choose a gender when we need pronouns. He or she? His or her? The construction of he/she or his/her is awkward and interrupts the flow of a sentence.

One idea, briefly in vogue in the nineties in business writing, was to alternate genders throughout a document. This was supposed to even out the references to male bosses and female secretaries. Instead, it just confused people. Who's the boss? Who's the secretary? Who's on first?

The funniest proposal for the pronoun problem is that we invent a genderless pronoun and use it to mean anything we want. I am not making this up—a rather serious man has suggested we call this pronoun *ze*. I wonder if ze has considered that, if ze goes around saying "ze," people will think ze is imitating Peter Sellers in ze Pink Panther movie?

Here is a typical example of a pronoun dilemma:

> The account executive must keep in touch with *his or her* clients.

And here are three practical suggestions for avoiding that gender problem in writing:

- Speak directly to the audience.

  As account executive, you must keep in touch with *your* clients.

- Take ownership away.

  The account executive must keep in touch with *the* clients.

- Make it plural—both subject and pronoun.

  All account *executives* must keep in touch with *their* clients.

Note that both must be plural. Don't say, "The account *executive* (singular) must keep in touch with *their* (plural) clients."

You can always find a way to write around gender references if you want to. I don't think the situation is so dire that we need to invent new pronouns. On the other hand, it would simplify the embroidery on towels (Ze and Ze), and it would give grammar geeks some new possibilities for using that Z tile in Scrabble.

Maybe not so good for the doors on public restrooms...

We Don't Need No
——————— Steenking Editors

(With apologies to the 1948 film classic, *The Treasure of Sierra Madre*)

I once interviewed for a job as Publications Director at a big home mortgage lender. The young, stylish female VP, more than an hour late, started the interview by berating her assistant in front of me. She continued to be condescending and unpleasant throughout the interview. When she got to the final question, I found myself in an editor's dream scenario. More on that later.

Editors are behind-the-scenes, unsung heroes who make others look good. They can be likened to the costumers and makeup artists who know the secrets of the stars they beautify. Who has hair extensions, who wears Spanx, who needs extra-heavy foundation. When editors get together, they invariably exchange stories of hilarious mistakes they've seen in print, corrected before they got there. Like the dozens of times someone has left the l out of *public*. I've seen that one so many times I'm starting to suspect people of doing it on purpose.

Often, the people who made these errors had no use for editors. Oh, the false sense of security when a spelling checker is all that stands between you and public embarrassment. And don't even get me started on Autocorrect.

Homophones, word pairs that are pronounced the same but have different spellings and different meanings, are tricky enough. But sometimes the word is spelled correctly although its usage is just plain wrong. I once knew a senior VP who was fond of these expressions:

> *recede* from the Union (slide off into the Gulf of Mexico?)

> we can't *waist* time (unless we spend it in the gym...)

> *carp* diem (sounded a little fishy, but I think he was just being koi. OK, I'll stop.)

These are the kinds of mistakes a good editor could have prevented. It's possible to be great at sales or managing or engineering—even writing—and still need the help of an editor. The price of salvation is just a little humility.

So what about the nasty woman who interviewed me? When she demanded, "What makes you think you have anything to offer us?" I offered, "I could protect you from mistakes like this," and handed her a highlighted printout from their website in which they discussed mortgage rates for **condoms**. That's right—instead of condos.

She shrieked, "Where did you get this?" I told her it was on her own company website. She insisted it was not, while frantically tapping on her computer, but the site came up and she saw that it was true. Without a word, she bolted from the room, presumably to lop off the head of the person who was responsible.

I let myself out. Who'd want to work for her anyway?

Over the River and
——————— Through the Woods

This traditional holiday song was written for people like me. I have no sense of direction and am notorious for getting lost. It's so bad that, years ago, my children gave me a GPS for Mother's Day.

Apparently, long before the GPS was invented, someone wrote the song to help us direction-impaired folks find the way to Grandma's house. The lyrics say that the horse knows the way, but what if he pulls up lame and you have a substitute horse? Hence the song.

Over, and then *through*—those prepositions give directions. They tell you where to go. Prepositional phrases are useful to clarify such concepts as *at the end of the street*, and *around the corner*, and *across the bridge*. But they can also become a bad writing habit. The results are often disconnected thoughts and long, tiresome sentences. They puff up your writing and make it fat.

As you seek ways to make your writing more concise, look first at the prepositional phrases. It's surprising how many can be eliminated without sacrificing meaning. Here is an example of a preposition-laden sentence (before) and its trimmed version (after).

Before

> Concerning your request from last week pertaining to one of the classes during this quarter for the most recent of our new products, we have room for no more than three of your employees until we open a new class because most of our instructors are out on the road and unavailable for us to assign them to additional classes on our schedule until next quarter.

After

> We appreciate your recent training inquiry. Currently, the class you requested can accommodate only three more students. As instructors' schedules permit, we will schedule more classes next quarter.

You'll notice the one long sentence is not only slimmed down, but it is also broken into three shorter ones. Each one contains a separate thought. It's not Shakespeare, but it communicates. If your goal is to get the message to your audience clearly, on the first try, consider this tip your own personal writing GPS.

As for getting to Grandma's house, you're on your own. She's probably at yoga class anyway.

Verbizing, Nounization,
——————————— and Pluralizings

I'm convinced that some disciplines suffer from jargon envy and that it starts in college. Education might be one of the worst, but it's easy to understand why. In a university coffee shop, you can hear math majors discussing concepts asymptotic, quadratic, Fibonacci, Cartesian, and polyhedral.

Music majors counterpunch with appoggiaturas, hemiolas, leggiermente, and vivacissimo. Not to be outdone, art majors unleash their intaglio, chiaroscuro, gouache, encaustic, and sgraffito.

But when the medical students swagger in, brandishing acetylcholinesterase, occipitotemporalis medialis, and paraskevidekatriaphobia, the place grows suddenly quiet with awe. It's like the scene in a cowboy movie when the bad guy walks into the saloon. Even the piano player stops. Med students are the undisputed champions of the jargon wars.

Is it any wonder that Education majors, who speak ordinary English most of the time, should want to baffle the uninitiated just like everyone else? It's the only explanation for making verbs out of perfectly good nouns, and then gerunds out of those verbs, and then plural nouns out of those gerunds... bringing us back to where we started, only longer and uglier. And if that isn't obtuse enough, they pile on the all-purpose adjective *cognitive*. It goes with everything.

Examples

> *dialog* (noun) -> *to dialog* (verb) -> *a dialoging* (gerund) -> *some dialogings* (plural noun)

> You should have frequent dialogings with the parents.

Haven't we come full circle? What was wrong with dialogs? Or even talks?

In many variations, educators (among others) love to add –ize and –ation and –ings to words that don't need them and shouldn't have them. It's as if more letters and syllables make these words esoteric and their meanings mysterious.

Just this week, I saw an ad for a company training series with multiple learnings.

> *learn* (verb) -> *learning* (gerund) -> *learnings* (plural noun)

Why not *courses* or *tutorials* or *lessons*? My favorite, though, was *CPU utilizings in Red Hat server...*

> *use* (verb) -> *utilize* (unnecessarily longer word) -> *utilizing* (gerund) -> *utilizings* (plural)

I don't know where to start with that one. Couldn't they just say *uses* in the first place?

There is nothing wrong with simple. Simple is smart. Simple is tasteful and elegant. This compulsion to complicate language smacks of trying too hard. It's a leopard print skirt with a zebra print blouse, gaudy jewelry, and a silly hat. It's the clown makeup of writing. What's next? Learningizings? Utilizingizations? It does nothing to help you communicate.

Beware. Don't let this happen to you. If you find yourself writing words with lots of added –izes, –ings, or –izations, it could be an early warning sign that you are helping to stupidificationize the language.

That's a Word? Seriously?

Technology, science, and pop culture provide a constant supply of new words for things that didn't exist yesterday. But some people always insist that English just needs a few more.

When I was a child, my father was on the local school board. In discussing plans for a new elementary school, the other board members insisted on calling the multi-purpose room the cafetorium (a combination of cafeteria and auditorium).

My dad, a stubborn sort, referred to it exclusively as the kitchenasium. He did it just to annoy them.

The intentional colorful or ironic use of made-up words can be fun. But several non-words have crept into such common usage that dictionaries are now—seriously—listing them as nonstandard or alternate spellings of legitimate words. There are vehement arguments on both sides of this question.

I never like to side with the stuffy, purist point of view if I can help it. But on a couple of these, I might line up with the defenders of the language. Even a certain silver-haired CNN star recently spoke of an escaped political prisoner who snuck into Shanghai. There is no such word as *snuck*, just as there is no such word as *irregardless*.

There is also no such word as *alls*, as in, "Alls I want is to go home."

These two always stir up a good debate:

> alot (for *a lot*)

> alright (for *all right*)

People swear they have seen them in ads (they have) and other types of writing (on the Internet?) so they must be— um—*all right*. Sadly, they are two signs of dumbing-down references that bow to common usage as arbiter. The fact that a lot of people say it does not make it all right. Otherwise, acceptable musical references for women would be determined by rap lyrics.

The combination of two polysyllabic words is always funny, whether it's a slip of the tongue or a genuine belief that it's a word:

- compenscate (compensate and confiscate)

- expotentially (exponent and potentially)

- ethenticity (ethnicity and authenticity)

- exonify (exemplify and personify)

- anticdote (anecdote and antidote)

So be careful. Unless you're using words like this in an ironic or humorous way, you're liable to be sentenced to detention after school.

In the kitchenasium.

Seriously.

Who, Whom, Whose,
and Who's

Sounds like a convention of owls, but questions about *who* and its variations apparently vex a lot of us. Even headline writers for major news services get it wrong.

Here are four expressions that have one thing in common— they are all wrong. Do you know why?

1. To who it may concern:

2. Whom do you think will be our next president?

3. Guess whose turning fifty.

4. Opening acts—Who's pre-Oscar style rules?

Few people would write the first one because the phrase "To whom it may concern..." is so familiar. But they might not transfer that principle to other writing. *Whom* is used when it's the object of a verb or a preposition.

Whom did you select to be on the new committee? (object of verb *select*)

Survivors included tourists, many of whom were children. (object of preposition *of*)

The #2 example should have been "Who do you think will be our next president" because it's the subject, not an object. If the sentence were diagrammed, you could see how it would function... but sentence diagramming seems to have gone the way of sock-darning. Other correct illustrations include:

Who wants ice cream? (sentence subject)

We may never know who that heroic man was. (subject of a clause)

The #3 example should be "Guess who's turning fifty." because it's a contraction for *who is*. Another example:

Who's Afraid of Virginia Woolf?

The #4 example is a headline I saw, in huge type, on an article about Academy Award nominees and their clothing choices. It should have been "Whose pre-Oscar style rules?" *Whose* means ownership, and is not a contracted form of *who is*. If you say, "Who is pre-Oscar style rules," it makes no sense at all. Unlike nouns, a pronoun doesn't form a possessive with an apostrophe and an s.

Whose fault is it that we have no food?

The proper form of *who* can leave you questioning what to write. You might find yourself backed into one of these corners:

(Who or whom) does the red jacket belong to?

(Whose or who's) jacket is the red one?

Don't despair. If you wonder who knows, to whom the jacket belongs, who's correct, and whose opinion is right, you can always just say, "Hey, does the red jacket belong to you?"

Let it Be

ood advice from the Beatles. Sometimes it's best to put vexing things aside and see how they look in the morning. Time, even a little, offers an amazing change in perspective.

For example, in high school everything is high drama. Teenage angst makes each disappointment seem like the end of the world. Many years ago, in the Midwest—context is important here—my first boyfriend was tall, cute, and exhibited pigs (excuse me… swine) at the county fair. He attended our biggest basketball-rival school, and I thought he was the love of my life. That is until he, you should pardon the expression, dumped me for a fertilizer heiress named Sue Ellen. I was devastated and vowed I would never smile again. I mean, I would never in my entire life be the daughter of a fertilizer magnate. And how can a girl compete with that?

Another high school friend of mine tells me that his prom date, whose dress was too poufy to fit into his Dodge, had to ride to the dance in the back of a pickup truck. Imagine today's teens dealing with that one. (No limo? I'm riding in a

WHAT?) At the moment they happened, these events seemed tragic, or at least humiliating. But in retrospect, they are deliciously funny. Such is the gift of time. Some things just take more time than others.

If you're having trouble with a piece of writing, let it rest for a few hours—or, if you can spare the time, days. Even if you are pleased with it, a new reading can give you fresh ideas and reactions. Sometimes words jump off the page and you think, "Did I write that?"

During composition, you're trying to communicate something that's already clear in your head. When you read your own writing too soon, you do so in that frame of mind. Your subconscious fills in gaps and clarifies what your words might have missed. After a rest, the writing goes cold, your mind is filled with other thoughts, and you look at it more objectively.

If you are editing your own work, even that process is better after some time passes. It is easy to write an awkward sentence or overlook a typo when your mind knows what you meant to say. The passage of a little time resets your thought processes and makes those mistakes easier to see. These are also good reasons not to fire off an angry email in haste. Let it sit and cool off. Save yourself possible embarrassment and regret.

So what ever happened to my first-love high school boyfriend? He earned an Agriculture degree in college, married the fertilizer heiress, and no longer raises pigs. But after all these years, I still giggle every time I think that he, an erstwhile connoisseur of fine swine, married a woman named *Suuuuuue E!*

Aaaahh—perspective.

Six Pack Abs in an Hour

Regrettably, we're not talking about physiques here. And, lest you think I'm some kind of fitness nut, I waited until my last baby graduated from college to start post-natal exercises. I didn't want to rush into anything.

TV, magazines, and the Internet are full of programs and secrets for the perfect lean, mean, athletic body, but achieving one is neither easy nor fast. Your writing is another matter.

Is your writing sluggish and flabby? Does it have volume but little energy? You can improve your writing today and still eat anything you want. Read on—it's free!

To tighten and tone your writing, let's target some problem areas. Many prepositions are little more than space fillers that add no value. They cause thunder-thighs and love handles. Trim several pounds right now and eliminate as many prepositional phrases as you can.

Here's another easy exercise: Examine your word choices. Obsolete business clichés, like commercial jingles, stick in our minds and they pop out when we can't think of anything else to say. These inflated expressions are just extra letters and syllables, empty calories that make you sound pompous. Think of them as eating doughnuts while lying on the sofa.

Although I don't recommend it, you could actually improve your writing while eating doughnuts and lying on the sofa. Choose lean words—the writing equivalent of healthful food and exercise.

Think of the words on the left as sugar and trans fats.

Think of the words on the right as vegetables.

- utilize—use

- at this point in time—now

- be of assistance to—help

- please do not hesitate to call us—call us

- due to the fact that—because

- during the time that—while

- have a preference for—prefer

- in spite of the fact that—although

- in the event that—if

- in the near future—soon

- in close proximity to—near

- it is highly recommended that you do this—do this

- enclosed please find—here is

All fitness gurus tell you there are no guarantees, but surveys show that you will see improvement if you follow this program. And when you admire sleek, beautiful, impossibly lean writing and think, "Mine could never look like that," just remember that most gorgeous published prose is air-brushed. By editors.

─────────────────────────── What is it?

I once worked at a large telecom company where everyone spoke in jargon. Some people understood it all, but many just pretended to. Although confusion was common, no one dared to ask what any of the words and acronyms meant. It just wasn't done.

My bright idea? A technical glossary website on the company intranet. Because it wasn't part of my job, I researched and wrote definitions on weekends, at night, during vacations, and on holidays. My glossary database grew to more than twenty thousand definitions and the site registered more than seventy thousand user sessions per month.

Co-workers exchanged knowing glances, hinting that I had an obsessive-compulsive disorder. The fools! They thought I was mad! (Insert evil laugh here.) But I learned how to write definitions.

Maybe you will never write a book that requires a glossary of terms. But someday you'll probably write a document or email in which you have to define something. A clear definition can be critical in communicating your message. Incomplete or ambiguous definitions leave your readers confused and irritated.

Some of the worst definitions are in sales and marketing literature, where you'd think a good definition of what you're selling is exactly the point. Here are four simple rules for writing a good definition:

1. First answer the question, "What is it?"

   Not its benefits, what it does, or how it's used. Is it a software application, a philosophy, a dessert topping, or a floor wax? Narrow it down—a synonym or a category—please.

2. Make it parallel.

   Build it like an algebraic equation. The equal sign means both sides have the same value. So use the same part of speech. A noun (thing) cannot be an adverbial phrase ("when something happens").

3. Don't repeat the term in the definition.

   Don't say, "breadbox—A breadbox is a box where you keep bread."

   Say, "breadbox—a container for storing baked goods."

4. Write in inverted pyramid style.

   State what it is, in one phrase, and then add
   what it does, how it's used, who invented it, or
   anything else the reader might find relevant.

Here is an example of how not to write a definition:

   SuperGreat Product—SuperGreat Product resulted when Swedish scientists responded to a
   common customer need. It is a product that is
   super and great and it leverages natural meth-
   odologies and is the answer to all of your problems. SuperGreat Product is such an effective
   solution that users report great results and a
   super-youthful appearance.

Is it a dietary supplement? A face cream? An exercise appa-
ratus? That one weird trick they're always talking about in
Internet ads? Is this starting to sound obsessive? I still don't
know what the <bleep> it is.

I wish I could tell you that I was known as the Glossary
Goddess at the telecom company, but you can't choose your
own nickname. I think my readers referred to me as the
Glossary Geek. It was as if, instead of definitions, I had
amassed twenty thousand baseball cards or comic books or
cats in my attic. Smirk all you want, but they did read those
definitions. In droves.

──────────── Dangers of Porch-sitting

This news report of an arrest in a small southern Indiana town concerns a well-known recording star's two teen-aged sons. We'll call them Shane and Bubba. The report stated:

> Shane and Bubba were charged with felony battery after allegedly beating up a man who was sitting on his front porch without warning.

There are lots of strange local ordinances in small Indiana towns, but I'd never heard of the requirement to announce your intention to sit on the front porch. Or that it could incite such violence. Seriously, the lesson here (one of them, at least) is that descriptive phrases must be near the word they modify. The *without warning* phrase should be close to *beating up*, for example:

> Shane and Bubba were charged with felony battery after allegedly, without warning, beating up a man who was sitting on his front porch.

This is the same mistake that causes misunderstandings and funny results, such as these classic favorites:

> For sale—Mahogany table by elderly lady with Chippendale legs.

> I don't care how bad her legs are as long as the table is in good condition.

It should be:

> For sale by elderly lady—Mahogany table with Chippendale legs.

This classic is silly:

> The waiter served toast to the young woman that was well buttered.

> Apparently her friend who was not well buttered got no toast.

It should be:

> The waiter served well-buttered toast to the young woman.

Misplaced modifying phrases often happen when you're trying to jam too much information into one sentence. The more you try to say, the longer, more complex, and more awkward the sentence becomes. Often, the best solution is to break it up into two shorter sentences expressing separate thoughts.

Now that you are aware of misplaced modifying phrases, you will be able to spot them in your own writing and correct them before they become the object of someone else's ridicule.

And, just to be safe, if you visit southern Indiana, remember: Before exiting through the front door, be sure to call out, "Warning—I'm going to sit on the front porch now."

─────────────── 4G Crosstalk

This topic has nothing to do with the version of your cell phone or wayward signals that wander onto the wrong circuit, mingling your bits and bytes with those of the Roto-Rooter dispatcher.

It's about four words, all beginning with the letter G, that many people confuse and misuse. If you find these words perplexing, you're not alone. Although the words have different meanings, even educated and literate people sometimes use them almost interchangeably, and thus incorrectly.

If you are unsure of their specific meanings, as most people are, you'd probably never correct others when they misuse them. Then again, maybe you're not the kind of person who would correct another's grammar anyway. In either case, this is your opportunity to win a bet with your brother-in-law, upstage that condescending co-worker, or just impress the Queen when she invites you to tea.

Working these words into a conversation is the hard part, but I will leave that to you:

- **Gantlet (or gauntlet)**—An old form of punishment, in which the victim was forced to run between two lines of people who flogged or beat him with sticks.

A modern-day version of this would be a middle school student, wearing last year's clothes, stepping off a school bus. Walking into the building between lines of cruel thirteen-year-old fashion critics would feel like running a gantlet.

- **Gauntlet** (but not gantlet)—A long glove worn by armored knights. To throw down the gauntlet was to issue a challenge to an adversary.

When someone throws a gauntlet, a fight ensues. In a western movie, the poker player who feels he's been cheated draws his gun and upends the poker table. That's a form of gauntlet-throwing.

- **Gamut**—An entire range or series of colors, sounds, or other qualities. Running the gamut means including everything from one extreme to the other.

In 1933, Dorothy Parker panned a famous actress by writing, "…she runs the gamut of emotions from A to B." Ouch.

- **Gambit**—An opening move, originally in chess, involving the surrender of something small in order to gain an advantage later.

Now used in negotiations and other general applications. If your child wanted to persuade you to take him to a movie, his opening gambit might be to clean his room—voluntarily.

Now that you are no longer confused about these four words, feel confident to run the gantlet of nay-sayers if they throw down a gauntlet to challenge you. Bring the entire gamut of your knowledge to the fight and emerge victorious, regardless of their opening gambit.

Everyone's a Tech Writer

You've probably been a technical writer, at least for a few minutes, at some time in your life. If anyone has ever asked you to write down how to get to the bus station, make a casserole, start a lawn mower, or turn off Autocorrect, you've composed instructions.

Tasks that seem easy to you can be baffling to someone else. Technical is in the eye of the beholder.

If you don't believe me, just order patio furniture online. Several large boxes arrive, each with a picture on the outside and printed instructions inside. Instructions that should help you assemble the furniture. But the text is only half translated, the steps are out of order, pieces are missing, or the instructions don't match the diagrams. The actual purpose of those instructions seems to be completing some manufacturing process checklist:

> ✓ Yes. Carton be comprise direction
>   in utilize by assemble object.

Terrible directions can make a proper librarian swear like a longshoreman. So here are some tips for writing good directions:

1. Number the steps.

2. Include all necessary information, but no more.

3. Use words the reader is likely to understand.

4. Write in clear, direct sentences beginning with active verbs.

5. Arrange the steps in correct order.

Some directions get this reaction: Wow. This writer must be really smart. I don't understand a word of that.

The reaction you want is: Wow. I can do this—it's not so hard.

Here's an example of what I'm talking about:

HOW TO GROW MAIDENHAIR FERNS INDOORS

Before

> The Adiantum raddianum is an attractive plant that may be grown indoors. Consistent watering, keeping the soil evenly moist is also key to the health and well-being of the plant. Overwatering causes fronds to yellow and wilt and may eventually lead to root rot, especially if the pot is allowed to sit in water. A

north-facing window is ideal although during the winter months, when the sun is low on the horizon, an east window is fine. Avoid south and west-facing windows, as the intense sunlight may scald the fronds, depending on the intensity of the light.

After

1. Place the plant in a warm spot with no direct sun.

2. Keep the soil moist, but don't let it sit in water.

3. Do not let it dry out. It will never forgive you.

4. Clip off the unattractive foliage with scissors every week or so.

5. Inspect the plant for foliage. When it has none left, buy a new plant.

Here's your chance to share your knowledge. If your instructions help someone solve a problem or complete a project, you've done a good deed.

Remember that some tasks are not as easy as assembling patio furniture. You can't always shout obscenities, throw away the directions, and just look at the picture on the box.

Repetitious, Unnecessary
———————————— Pleonasms

There's an interesting word for you—*pleonasm*. You know what it is, but perhaps you never attached this name to it. It's the use of redundant words that inflate your writing. Pleonasms are sometimes colloquial, and often just reflect casual speech patterns, but they cause trouble when they creep into your writing.

Spellchecker won't catch them, and many grammar checkers won't flag them as wrong. So you're on your own.

Legalese has to cover every possibility, so it is full of them— *null and void; cease and desist; will and testament; irrelevant, irresponsible, and immaterial*—but legal language is hardly an example of clear and efficient writing. If writing were a person, legalese would be that eleven hundred-pound guy on TV who hasn't left his bedroom in years and has to have a wall removed because he can't fit through the door.

Think of pleonasms as the cholesterol that clogs the arteries of your writing, slowing its flow and making it sluggish. Lethargic and bloated are not attractive images. Before you publish or distribute any piece of writing, examine it for pesky pleonasms.

Here are some I've seen recently, how they might be improved, and why they're wrong:

- He looked at her with those green eyes of his

  He looked at her with those green eyes.

  (He couldn't look with anyone else's eyes, could he?)

- I'll have a tuna fish sandwich.

  I'll have a tuna sandwich.

  (Tuna is a fish. You don't order a chicken poultry sandwich.)

- ATM machine

  ATM

  (The M stands for machine.)

- I need new eye glasses.

  I need new glasses.

  (Where else would you wear them?)

- Click here for your free gift.

  Click here for your gift.

(That's what a gift is—something free.)

- He's a personal friend.

  He's a friend.

  (There's an impersonal friend?)

- This idea is quite unique.

  This idea is unique.

  (*Unique* is an absolute, with no comparatives.)

- It was a tiny speck.

  It was a speck.

  (If it were large, it wouldn't be a speck.)

- She's a widow woman.

  She's a widow.

  (If she were a man, she'd be a widower.)

- We commuted back and forth to the city every day.

  We commuted to the city every day.

  (*Commuted* means traveled back and forth.)

- She descended down the staircase.

She descended the staircase.

(It's impossible to descend up a staircase.)

* I think I'll buy these ones

I think I'll buy these.

(The idea of ones or items is implied in *these*.)

We're all guilty of occasional pleonasms. Remember to look for them if you need to fit some text into a tweet, a newsletter column, a website box, or a restricted field.

Don't be the person who writes like this:

> Be absolutely sure that you labor diligently over each and every single word you write so that the true facts are not obscured and hidden by the redundant, repetitive, tautological, unnecessary phrases and verbiage and groups of words. Make completely sure that every single word is absolutely necessary as a component part of the composition you have written and supports its ultimate goal. It should be visible with your own eyes that, if you are vacillating back and forth between alternative choices, literate readers will be sadly disappointed that your very own writing is so inflated and wordy and verbose.

How many pleonasms can you find?

——————— Dead. Definitely Dead.

D eath makes people uncomfortable. They don't know how to say it, and they just don't want to talk about it.

One of my favorite comedy bits is the classic Monty Python Dead Parrot Sketch. In its many variations, a customer tries to convince a pet store owner that the parrot he's been sold is dead.

When the shopkeeper makes excuses, the frustrated customer insists (with every euphemism imaginable) that the parrot is dead. Paraphrased, his rant goes something like this:

> "Dead. Definitely deceased. Bleeding demised. Passed on. No more. Ceased to be. Expired and gone to meet its maker. Late. Stiff. Bereft of life. Resting in peace. Pushing up the daisies. Rung down the curtain and joined the choir invisible. This is an ex-parrot!"

Euphemisms for *dead* occur on news reports of tragic events—accidents, disasters, murders—any event in which life is lost.

One of the most common is *deceased*. The word *deceased* is just dead with four extra letters. It's like utilize instead of use. Deceased sounds most appropriate when it's describing provisions of a will. The Deceased is the person who has bequeathed something to the Beneficiaries.

But law enforcement personnel, interviewed on camera at the scene of a homicide, rarely use the word *dead*. They are more likely to describe the situation like this:

> "Officers entered the residence at 2:13 p.m. and found two Caucasian males in their early twenties who were deceased..."

I understand that cop-speak requires a standard vocabulary for legal reasons. Police officers can't call a perpetrator a scumbag, even if they know he did it. They have to refer to him as a suspect or—this is hilarious—sometimes even a gentleman.

> "The entire family is deceased. We found this gentleman standing over them, covered in blood, screaming obscenities at police, and waving a large machete..." (Does that describe the behavior of a gentleman?)

Civilian witnesses and news reporters sometimes try to mimic the manner of police when they're asked about a tragic event. Another term they like to use is *passed away*.

> "Yeah, we heard gunshots and then we just found him here, passed away, on the sidewalk..."

Passed away seems more fitting for a quiet end to a long illness in a hospital than violent murder on the street.

If dead sounds too blunt, how about these alternatives?

Seven people did not survive the crash.

First responders found him, lifeless, on the floor.

All three succumbed to their injuries.

A thirty-two-year-old woman, the victim of an apparent homicide...

Attempts to revive him failed.

The storm has claimed twenty-seven lives.

Three people were fatally wounded.

He lost his life while trying to save his friend.

But enough with the deceased and passed away. This is sufficient. End of discussion. I'm over it. Enough already. Subject is exhausted. My two cents. No more to say. I have spoken. It is over. We're done here. Finito. This is an ex-topic.

Shouting About Readability!!!

Although much has been written about this, some people still think you can emphasize a thought by writing it in all capital letters. I often see instructions, e-mails, and entire paragraphs written all in caps. But all-caps is actually a barrier to reading and comprehension.

Here's a tip if you have to give a presentation or a speech, and you don't want to wear your reading glasses. Don't print your script in all-caps. It will be almost impossible to read. Print it in a larger font than normal (maybe fourteen points and boldface if you like), but with normal sentence capitalization.

When a client recently gave me one hundred twenty-eight pages of rules and regulations to edit, all in capital letters, he said, "I thought it would make it seem more important." (For now, we'll just ignore the question of how, in on hundred twenty-eight pages, all of the information can be equally important...) All-caps is a known readability killer. So why would anyone use it on purpose?

Consider this illustration:

Upscale restaurants, where meals are expensive, service is excellent, and tips are expected to be generous, tend to provide comfortable surroundings. Pleasant ambience, soft lighting, music, soothing color schemes. Take your time and enjoy the dining experience. They make their money on markup.

Fast food places with cheap meals, no service, and no tips, want you to finish eating and leave—so they can turn your table over to another customer. They give you hideous orange vinyl booths, harsh fluorescent lighting, and lots of noise. It's not because they can't afford good interior designers, and it's no accident of décor... it's an environment that makes you anxious and uncomfortable. So you will leave. They make their money on volume.

The connection? The fast food joint doesn't want you to linger. In fact, it would suit them just fine if you gathered your burgers and fries and ate them in your car. Think about the last time you did not want to take the time to read something. Was it one of those Terms and Conditions statements that everyone clicks through without reading? Now think back... I guarantee at least one large section, if not all of it, was written in all caps.

If it's just one section, it's most likely the disclaimer or the part about liability. And the reason? They don't want you to read it. Reading all caps feels as if someone is shouting at you and it's laborious. You're supposed to move on and agree to the terms, but not read them.

People violate readability rules all the time, and they wonder why their writing is not successful. Here are some other factors that inhibit readability, especially if the text is more than three or four words. The longer the text, the greater the effect.

Block justification

> That feature that evens out the right   margin,
> resulting in white spaces between some words
> scattered throughout a paragraph, for no
> apparent reason, or odd white   space
> in a   very   short   line.

Italics

> *For emphasis, an italicized font is fine. For a pretty,*
> *decorative title it's fine. Anything involving just a few*
> *words, it's fine. But if you have very much to say,*
> *italics have the opposite effect from the one you*
> *might want. Instead of emphasizing a point, it makes*
> *the reader want to stop reading.*

Small fonts

> It's not rocket science that tiny type will cause many readers to give up. If you have so much to say that
> it will not fit into the space, shorten the message so you can use a larger font. Otherwise, the poor reader
> will be squinting and adjusting his glasses and probably getting a massive headache.

Lack of contrast

> Some artistic layouts look great when you treat blocks
> of text as art objects. But if the background is light
> gray and the text is medium gray and you use shadows
> and gradients, your reader will have a difficult time
> figuring out what you're trying to say.

Scripty, scrolly fonts

> *For a title or a logo, one or two words might be O.K.
> But if you want people to read an entire paragraph of
> something written in a decorative font, just know that they
> won't bother. If your lovely party invitation is hard to
> read, people might not come on the right day, or at all.*

With so much content presented online in recent years, some of the old rules of readability have changed slightly. But the most readable fonts are still at least ten points or so. First-cap-only (called sentence case) is still more readable than all caps, even for titles or headings. Definitely for entire paragraphs. So the next time you're tempted to write something in all caps, imagine that burger clown shouting,

"HEY—HURRY UP AND GET OUT OF HERE!
WE WANT TO GIVE YOUR HIDEOUS
ORANGE VINYL BOOTH TO SOMEONE ELSE!
OH YEAH, AND HAVE A NICE DAY!"

How much better to say, "Welcome. Your table is waiting… enjoy your meal."

—————— Using the Right F Word

Seriously now, you didn't think I meant that, did you? I'm talking about two word pairs that people often confuse, especially in business conversations.

flesh out or flush out?

and

farther or further?

Picture a planning session. The presenter says we needed to *flush out* an outline, when he means to add detail. Suddenly, I can't focus on the proposal. That mental picture of the project in a toilet bowl, swirling its way down to the sewer... does the speaker know he has just suggested discarding the whole plan?

People who use *flush out* in this way mean *flesh out*, as in adding meat to the bones (or skeleton) of the plan. There is no room for debate on this one. Flush out, in this situation, is always wrong. Flesh out is the phrase to use when you mean that you have a framework, and now you need to develop it further—or is it farther?

That brings me to the next word pair dilemma: *farther* or *further*. Traditionally, farther has been used in describing distance:

> The finish line is farther away than I thought.

Further has been used in a metaphorical or abstract sense:

> Let's explore this idea a little further.

These are still good general rules, and you can remember that farther contains the word *far*, as in measurable, physical distance. But the distinction between the two words has become so hazy that even experts disagree. Many usage cases are ambiguous and it's hard to be sure which rule applies.

Here is an example:

> Building this wall is such hard work, I don't
> want to continue any (farther or further?).

The length of the wall represents a physical distance, but the amount of effort required is abstract. Unless it's clearly a measure of distance, *further* is the safer choice. No reasonable person will criticize you for using either word here.

So, farther down the road, if you're discussing your great idea in an attempt to flesh out your plan, and someone says you should flush it out, just collect your things, leave, and refuse to discuss it any further.

Just-wrong-enough
———————————— Word Choices

You're only a letter or two off. And besides, everyone knows what you mean anyway. Is close enough really good enough? I'm not talking about obvious errors, but subtle word choices that might go mostly unnoticed.

I realize some will accuse me of being picky or pedantic, as if it all doesn't matter anyway. But when you force your audience to figure out what you mean, you're being lazy and weakening your writing.

Educated people do it. Professionals and successful business people do it. They are understood, for the most part, and some people even consider them articulate. But their glib communication leaves an almost-there, not-quite-right, about-seven-degrees-off-center feeling. They use big words and they seem smart, but there's just something you can't put your finger on...

Although you probably know what these sentences mean, each one contains a wrong word choice:

- I expect you and your brother to behave respectively at Grandma's house.

  Problem—Respectively means in the order given. It means that you take turns behaving. First you behave, then your brother behaves. What—? Each of you is also free to misbehave as long as you take turns? The proper word is *respectfully*, which means with deference and courtesy.

- Many accidents occur where these two major streets intercept.

  Problem—Unless you're discussing Cartesian coordinates, *intercept* as a verb generally means to stop or interrupt a path, such as that of a message or a football pass, that was intended for someone else. Two streets intersect—cut across or overlap each other. That's why a street corner is called an intersection, not an interception.

- We hope all of you will partake in the festivities.

  Problem—Partake contains the words *take* and *part*, but it does not mean *take part*. It's usually followed by the word *of,* and means to consume or eat. You partake of the appetizers and you partake of the barbecue. But you participate in the festivities. You can't eat a festivity.

Why does this matter?

Your readers and listeners unravel these subtle errors in flight, probably without even realizing it. But the brain takes a detour and registers "Huh?" while it should be using its processing power to hang on your every word or agree with your point. While the reader's brain is busy creating new neural pathways around the blunder, you've moved on to a new point. The slightly wrong choices suggest fuzzy thinking and flawed logic.

Precise word choices enable your audience to focus on your message with confidence. They are easy to digest. Careful, on-target nouns and verbs add strength to your writing and speaking, and they reward you with trust and credibility.

Tune in

Public figures who work from prepared speeches sometimes reveal their true nature when they wander off-book or appear in interviews where there is no speech writer. Listen for word choices the next time you hear a speech, a presentation, or a debate. The speaker might be seeking your vote, your money, or your agreement on a business matter. And once you tune in to it, you'll find it difficult to support fuzzy thinking.

Sadly, I respectfully submit that listening too closely can discourage voting. As the democratic process intersects with the "close enough" mentality, we all participate in the resulting dilemma:

Of all the candidates, presenters, and colleagues, whose thinking is the least fuzzy?

Five Reasons To Use
—————— Numbers in Headlines

Everyone knows you should stuff numbers into your head-lines. If you do, people can't resist reading the article. Often they're disappointed, but—hey—they read the ar-ticle and that's the most important part. Right?

It's not a new technique, but it has reached ridiculous levels of usage online. The Internet rewards clicks without regard to the quality or usefulness of the content. We all know that, so why do we fall for it?

Because we just can't help ourselves. Here are the *top five reasons people use numbers in their headlines:

1. They sound specific.

    A numbered list of steps will lead you directly to the solution you want. Whatever it is you're looking for, you've found the answer and it's right here!

2. They promise small chunks.

   No long paragraphs to read, probably no big words, and lots of white space. What could be easier to scan, skim, and digest? (Or write?)

3. People count to ten better than they read.

   Even a generation of TV-watching children who have never read a book can recognize the numbers one to ten. It's how many fingers they have.

4. They make complex tasks sound simple.

   If it can be reduced to a short, numbered list, how hard can it be? No education necessary, no boring tests—even you could do it!

5. They make the information seem credible.

   As if it were the result of research or some kind of controlled study. It's actually anything you want to make up to fit the number you wanted to put in the headline.

   The claim *top five reasons I used earlier? I just made that up. Who's going to argue that there are four reasons? Or six?

Be sure to read my next article entitled *Five Steps to Performing an Apendectomy.* Spoiler alert—the steps are:

1. Anesthetize patient

2. Make small incision over the appendix

3. Locate appendix

4. Remove it

5. Close incision

Easy.

—————————— Apostrophe Apoplexy

We almost expect to see misspelled words and misused apostrophes in hand-lettered signs selling fruit. It's as if there's an unwritten rule that delicious, home-grown fruit requires a lack of attention to spelling or punctuation.

Fresh cantalope's by the side of the road seem to taste better than fresh cantaloupes you can buy at any old grocery store.

The rules for plurals and possessives are pretty simple and apply to a majority of cases:

Noun	Possessive
dog (singular)	dog's
dogs (plural)	dogs'

Plaintiffs's?

A legitimate industry magazine says, "HP and respected *plaintiffs's* lawyers entered into an agreement..." Not just a typo, it occurs three times in the article. Someone did that on purpose. The word *plaintiffs* was already plural and required only an apostrophe to make it possessive.

Try to say *plaintiffs's* three times without sputtering.

Lex'

To make a plural, add an s. To make a possessive, add an apostrophe and an s. If only life were that simple. How about nouns that already end in s or es? Or ss? Or z or x? How do we make them plural and possessive, and how about the apostrophe? That's when it all goes terribly wrong.

Lex, a beloved member of a local tennis club died tragically. The well-meaning club management remodeled and renamed the bar in his honor. Emblazoned on the window in neon for years, it said Lex' instead of Lex's. If his name had been Joe, it would have said Joe's. But the x threw everyone.

I knew Lex, a literate man. I always imagined him looking down with reluctant disapproval… touched by the tribute, but embarrassed by the error.

Some exceptions send you running to your trusty *Chicago Manual of Style*, but here are some general examples:

Singular	Possessive	Plural	Plural possessive
Mr. Jones	Mr. Jones's car	The Joneses	The Joneses' house
Groucho Marx	Groucho Marx's cigar	The Marxes	The Marxes' movies
princess	The princess's tiara	Both princesses	Both princesses' gowns

Just cheat

Above all, don't agonize over this one. The difficult cases are perfect opportunities for writing around the problem. For example, let's say you need to write:

> For (appearance' or appearance's) sake, don't post (James' or Jameses'), (Moises' or Moiseses), or (Elvis' or Elvis's) test scores.

You can say this:

> For the sake of appearance, don't post test scores for James, Moises, or Elvis.

Then take the rest of the day off.

Tag—You're It

In Tag, the *it* person tags the closest victim, whoever that might be. If you're *it*, you don't run around searching for someone in particular. Anyone will do.

An introductory phrase is like the *it* person in that childhood game. It appears first in a sentence and is followed by a comma. It attaches itself to the closest noun or pronoun after the comma, and that's the one it modifies.

Sometimes the intended target is far away, later in the sentence or hiding behind a tree, but that's another game.

When the word described by the introductory phrase appears at the end of the sentence, with other nouns in the way, the results can be surprising and comical. Here are three examples I have seen—in print—from people who write for a living.

1. Being a fan of the book, the movie was so disappointing.

   Literal meaning—The movie was a fan of the book.

2. As a pediatric physician, each patient is very important to me.

   Literal meaning—Each of my patients is a pediatric physician.

3. Under the influence of a controlled substance with a prior, officers arrested the man.

   Literal meaning—Officers were under the influence of drugs, and the drugs had a prior.

The third one is a double disaster. Inside the introductory phrase there's a prepositional phrase (*with a prior*) that's also misplaced.

Here are the same examples, rewritten to make sense:

1. Being a fan of the book, I found the movie disappointing.

2. As a pediatric physician, I consider each patient very important.

3. Under the influence of a controlled substance and with a prior, the man was arrested by officers.

In each case, the subject immediately follows the comma after the introductory phrase. Example 3 is still awkward, and would be clearer like this:

   Officers arrested the man, who was under the influence of a controlled substance and also had a prior.

> **Always beware of introductory phrases and the first noun that follows them.**

Carelessly writing your introductory phrases, readers might tag the wrong noun.

Taking Out the Fluff

Fluff has its place. Kittens, down comforters, meringue desserts. But it's a readability-killer when it creeps into your writing. I don't know whether Writing Fluff is taught in business schools or whether it's something Marketing majors learn on the street. Either way, there's too much of it out there.

So what—you ask—is fluff in writing? Anything that adds unnecessary volume without adding meaning. Adjectives, adverbs, gerunds, prepositional phrases, long sentences. In a misguided attempt to say everything, fluff writers succeed only in obscuring the message they're trying to convey.

Much marketing copy reads as if four people sat around a table and collaborated on a pitch. The goal was to say everything they could think of about the product in one sentence. One by one, each person contributed a word or a thought until the sentence reached the optimum level of fluffiness. Here is an actual example from ABC company (not its real name), where I once worked:

Only ABC provides an approach that uniquely brings information, processes and people together in a dynamic case-based application that leverages ABC's unique strength in analytics to help optimize case outcomes, while leveraging the broadest ecosystem of available business-ready solutions and richest portfolio of enterprise software capabilities.

I can just hear them asking, "Did we say *unique* enough?" and "How about *optimize, leverage,* and *ecosystem?*" "Wait! We forgot *dynamic* and *solutions!*" Meanwhile, if you made it to the end of this convoluted sentence, chances are you lost track of what they're selling. Hint—It's case management software.

It can be fun to create a fluff-filled sentence as an exercise, as long as you don't try to use it on the public. Here's a fictitious horrible example. Can you guess what business it is?

Only XYZ provides a dazzling array of wonderfully diverse herbaceous comestibles including salubrious tubers, rhizomes, and legumes, but not to the exclusion of salutary tree-bearing seed-associated structures in a variety of species utilizing all the processes of modern agribusiness to the exclusion of irresponsible application of biocides, nematicides, and other pathogens which may or may not affect the overall level of functional or metabolic efficiency of living organisms.

Answer—Organic fruit and vegetable stand. Makes your mouth water, doesn't it?

Not To Be. That Is
―――――――――――――――――――― the Answer.

Shakespeare's Hamlet uttered, "To be or not to be, that is the question… " in a despondent mood. Questioning his own will to live, he wallowed in despair with no economy of expression whatsoever. In fact, he rather went on and on about it.

If you wrote that speech today, people would accuse you of being paid by the word.

Poetic, lyrical writing still exists, but most of us write for more practical reasons. Non-artistic writing communicates. It persuades, educates, warns, or amuses its audience. Everyday writing includes news reports, business communications, emails, web pages, social media posts, advertising, and a host of other categories. Although different from each other, all types work better when they're concise.

The various ways to make your writing more concise could fill a book. In fact, they have filled several. Some of these books, ironically, are not concise at all. But you can start looking for a common culprit in your own writing today—forms of the verb *to be*.

In English, *to be* verb forms include *is, was, are, were, have been, is being,* and *am being,* for example. Any sentence beginning with *There* (as in *There are...* or *There is...*) can be improved. Although *that* is not always involved, it's often a telltale sign.

Before—There are some issues that the committee is not going to consider until next week.

After—The committee postponed some issues until next week.

Before—There were so many movies that were good to choose from that we could not decide which one to see.

After—We could not decide which of the many good movies to see.

Before—Whenever there were controls that were lifted, there was chaos and rampant bad behavior.

After—Chaos and bad behavior followed the elimination of controls.

To be verb forms often function as filler words. They leave the impression you're avoiding or postponing the point of the sentence. Concentrate on the subject and what you want to say about it. Then just say it.

Will this tip protect you against all the slings and arrows of outrageous fortune? No, but it will give you some arms against a sea of troubles. You just have to practice and learn how to use it. Aye, there's the rub.

Communication
—— with Evil Intent

News flash! Some people are not nice. Many are deceptive, slick, selfish, and mean—on purpose, with malice aforethought. And most of them don't care if they hurt you. Fortunately, most of them adopt habits and behaviors you can spot if you're paying attention. If you know how to detect dishonesty, you're better able to protect yourself or counteract it.

Individuals aren't the only entities that systematically employ deception. Businesses do it at a high level with the government and consumers, and they do it internally with their own employees. Some of the techniques are relatively harmless, but others can affect your career.

The last essay in this section, *Truth Cards*, is less about malicious dishonesty than about things you'd like to say in greeting cards, in defiance of the greeting card industry, which has forced us to lie and be nice even when we don't want to be.

Warning—Deception
—————————————— Ahead

It's never easy to say something critical, even when we try to convince ourselves the criticism is constructive. Few people accept negative comments about themselves well, even if some have learned to put on a good face and pretend it doesn't sting.

But introducing your criticism with an obvious qualifier does nothing to soften the blow. In fact, it puts the receiver on the alert and casts you as both wimpy and disingenuous. In the worst cases, bullies use these phrases to make themselves feel less guilty. As if they provide license to say something no one should say.

Eliminate these introductory phrases from your vocabulary and realize that each one communicates exactly the opposite of the thought that follows.

- *With all due respect*, that's the ugliest design I've ever seen. (Where's the respect in that?)

- *No offense*, but no one wears that style anymore. (That's not offensive?)

- *To be perfectly honest,* the documents must have been lost in the mail. (Really? Or stolen by aliens?)

- *If you want to know the truth,* I have always supported your candidacy. (Would a politician lie?)

- *It's nothing personal,* but you just aren't someone I want to spend my life with. (How much more personal could it be?)

- *This is for your own good...* I think you should give up on your dreams. (Thanks for the encouragement.)

- *Don't take this the wrong way,* but you really need to lose some weight. (There's a right way to take that?)

- *Others are saying, not that I agree,* that you're aloof and condescending. (If you disagree with them, why are you telling me?)

I've heard every one of these qualifiers in both personal and business interactions. People say them to fill space before delivering a message they know, or should know, is going to hurt—or before telling a blatant lie. Be aware of how they sound and promise me you won't use them. I'm all for getting along and being nice. But if someone uses one of these on you, feel free to respond and call them on it.

All due respect? But what you said was disrespectful. No offense? Sounds pretty offensive to me. Take it the wrong way? No, I think you don't want me to take it the right way.

If this tactic results in a physical threat to you, I hope you are bigger than the offender and have martial arts training. If not, I hope you run fast and have a head start. Because if you want to know the truth, and this is for your own good, a clever retort does little to disarm a bully.

How To Be a Weasel

D isclaimer—This is satire. Do not try this at home. Before reading on, raise your right hand, place your left hand on a copy of Strunk and White, and repeat after me, "I (insert your name) solemnly promise to use this information for good, and not to benefit the forces of evil."

This is about negative example. It's what people do when they are trying to deceive you or hide the truth. These are techniques to avoid—assuming you're an honest person and not a lying weasel. Do not confuse this with Mountweazel, an entirely different thing. A Mountweazel is a kind of Easter egg deliberately placed in a reference work to detect plagiarism or copyright infringement.

But back to weasels.

Here are some clues that suggest the writer or speaker is being sneaky or untrustworthy:

- Qualifiers—allegedly, reportedly, arguably, probably, somewhat, in some respects...

- Passive verbs—it was decided, done, said, rumored, suggested, recommended...

- Euphemisms—downsizing (instead of layoffs), non-performing assets (instead of overdue debts), pre-owned (instead of used)...

- Multiple negatives—I did not say I would never..., It hasn't been disproven that..., Outlaws the prohibition of...

- Long sentences, complicated constructions, pompous pseudo-legal language—Note herein the multiple references to the aforementioned party and all property due the said parties heretofore mentioned, notwithstanding any previous provisions made subsequent to the current agreement...

- Triplet constructions—created, caused, and resulted in..., disregarded, neglected, and abandoned..., discontinue, cease, and desist...

- Lots of Latin—bona fide, ad hoc, in absentia, per se, de facto, ex officio, prima facie...

You, of course, would never employ any of these practices. But you will probably read them. They are all ways to shade or camouflage a truth instead of stating it directly. Although one of these clues does not automatically mean the writer is being deceptive, more than one of them should sound an alarm in your head and put you on alert. Be aware that this alert condition can cause increased heart rate, elevated blood pressure, and hyperventilation.

So consider yourself warned. It's probably wise to consult a physician before reading any legal documents or ballot propositions. And if anyone you know actually talks like this, run for your life.

Seven Habits of Highly
Effective Trolls

The Urban Dictionary says a troll is…. "one who posts a deliberately provocative message to a newsgroup or message board with the intention of causing maximum disruption and argument."

If you're a genuine troll, you aren't reading this. If you're not a troll, I don't need to tell you how infuriating trolls can be and how hard it is to refrain from reacting to what they—um—write. (I was going to write *spew*, but I'm trying to be nice.)

What I can do is warn you about troll-like habits that can creep into the writings of reasonable people, especially when the topic is controversial or emotional.

If you don't want to be mugged, don't walk alone in a bad part of town late at night. Likewise, avoid any site or discussion group known to be a free-for-all for crazies, right? But recently, even respectable business discussion groups have begun to show the signs of urban decay. It's not safe to walk anywhere these days. The habits of trolls have made us forget what civilized—and effective—discussion is like.

The following examples are largely compiled from discussions on a legitimate business site that shall remain nameless. Here's how to guarantee that readers will dismiss you as a troll:

1. Ignore punctuation.

   cuz nobody cares if you know where commas go anyways thats not important what is this english class I don't think its as important as having really good ideas and who are you to tell me what to do

2. Forget about grammar and spelling.

   Just between you and I, me and him don't car there all a bunch of whinners oh boo hoo

3. Jump to crazy conclusions.

   So if you think we should be nice two each other, you probly support the law that makes it illegal too give negative feedback in a performance evaluation... oo let's all go to jail!

4. Ramble and repeat yourself.

   This is the worst idea ever who cars about writing anyways. Its a really bad idea. We definately shouldnt due this because it's a not-good, super-wrong, cockamaimy idea. Who had this bad idea? I know someone who has this idea and she is stupid. Also she is ugly. Shes fat and ugly and who cars what she thinks.

5. Be defensive and sarcastic.

Oh yeah? Well I suppose you think anyone who can't write a decent sentence should be fired. Great—let's all just pack up are belongings and leave the building. Somebody call the grammer police!

6. Engage in juvenile name-calling.

Oh grab a tissue and just grow up, you big baby. What are you, in kindygarden? You sissy bleeding-hearts make me sick. If you wimps had your way we would all be commies.

7. SHOUT IN ALL-CAPS!

OUR FREEDOM TO BE IDIOTS IS IN DANGER! DON'T YOU PEOPLE GET IT? WE'RE ALL GONNA DIE!!!!

People exchange opinions in many ways. In business, in personal communication, and lots of places outside Internet discussion groups. Email, social media, even the back-and-forth of business proposals and responses. Most of these exchanges are civil and mutually respectful. But people resort to bullying behavior when they run out of reasoned arguments. So it's often a signal that they're losing the debate and have no good responses left.

Although exaggeration makes a point, no exaggeration is necessary to show you how troll-like habits kill your message and turn readers against you—even if they agree with your position.

Despite what the trolls tell you, the way you present your argument has a lot to do with whether readers consider it or discard it. And the best way to disarm a troll is to just click... <Delete>

Double Negatives
———————————— Are a No-No

When you hear *double negative*, do you think of a country bumpkin who says "I ain't got no..." and "It don't make me no nevermind?" You might be surprised to know how many people think they're using a classier form of double negative to sound smart.

Or—wait a minute—maybe it's to avoid saying something else. Something that would be clearer if stated positively.

The worst examples, ballot propositions, contain so many switchbacks that voters can't figure out whether they're for or against them. "Vote yes to prevent restriction on limitations of the governor's ability to veto any measure that blocks a moratorium on non-voter-approved prohibitions..." No wonder voters avoid the polls in off-year elections.

Grammatically correct double negatives raise more questions than they answer. That's why people in certain lines of work <cough> *con-men and politicians* <cough> use them. But real people use them too. Consider these examples:

- She's really not unattractive, unintelligent, or unsophisticated.

Does that mean she is attractive, intelligent, and sophisticated? Or just that she's not completely ugly, stupid, and common? There's a huge gray area between those two possibilities. Would you rather the man in your life described you as beautiful or not totally hideous?

- I'm not opposed to the idea...

So, does that mean you're for it? Would you stand by and watch it happen, vote for it, or support it? Would you approve funding for it?

- I didn't say I would not consider...

But you also didn't say you would. And the fact that you didn't say it means nothing.

- It is not incorrect to assume that...

Not-wrong does not always equal right, just as not guilty doesn't necessarily mean innocent. Many jurors have said, after delivering a not guilty verdict, "We all think he did it. There just wasn't enough evidence to put him away for life."

Everyone indulges in wishful thinking and denial. We believe the best in people and we want positive outcomes. So when we hear two negative expressions that seem to cancel each other, we're all too eager to accept it as a positive. But maybe it's just a slimy way for the speaker to not exactly say yes. It leaves the door open for back-pedaling later, as in,"What I actually said was..."

Beware of these self-cancelling double negatives in business negotiations and personal exchanges. If you encounter one in an important discussion, ask for a restatement in positive terms. The speaker will either commit to a positive stance or change the subject. If the speaker refuses to let the statement be clarified, you have your answer. How would you interpret this conversation?

John: Marsha, you're the love of my life. Will you marry me?

Marsha: John, you know I'm nothing if not fond of you. Our time together has not been unpleasant. The idea of spending my life with you is not disagreeable, and I'm not saying I wouldn't like to do that. Our attraction is not unlike that of Romeo and Juliet. When people say we're not meant for each other, I never fail to disagree with them. It would not be incorrect to say that I am not opposed to the idea.

John, old buddy, if you think that's a yes, I hope you kept the receipt for the ring.

Purgers and
Hack-quisitions

You work for a small-to-medium-sized company, and you're the ideal employee with outstanding performance reviews. Congratulations! Your small-fish company has just been gobbled up by a much larger one.

At last you don't have to explain to people who your employer is, because everybody knows. It's a household name. Salary and benefits are good. This could be your big break, the beginning of a stellar career that shoots you to the top of the corporate ladder. Or not.

Don't rush out and get new headshots for your *Forbes* cover just yet.

You might glide into a long-term career with the new company, but update your résumé and reactivate your network of contacts just the same. The corporate welcome sounds encouraging at first, and you will be tempted to believe it. But—guaranteed—all company communication comes right out of a playbook.

Huge companies acquire smaller ones for a number of reasons. Taking on hundreds (or thousands) of redundant employees is not one of them. It might not happen immediately, but within two or three years, staff will be reduced. Over time, fewer and fewer of your original colleagues will remain.

It's easy to lay off an entire department of worker bees. Just reorganize, eliminate their job functions, and give everyone a token severance package. But middle managers making good salaries are a little more of a problem. The formula is to assign them the dirty work (firing lower-level employees) and caution them not to say "I'm sorry" because it creates a potential vulnerability in case of litigation. They must tell the employee that the firing decision was theirs alone and they were not pressured by the company. Many managers don't have the stomach for this. If some still won't leave, axe them in the next round of layoffs.

So how do you survive if your company is acquired? Above all, don't believe everything you hear. Here is the communications code for surviving a major acquisition:

We bought your company because we value all of you terrific people. [We bought you to get your client list, patents, infrastructure, customer base, wireless spectrum, to fill a hole in our product line, to remove you from the competition...]

We are not planning any personnel changes right now. [We'll wait until the dust settles in order to minimize the bad press when we let most of you go. We have deep pockets and we can afford to wait.]

You're part of our family now. [We never forget who came in through acquisitions. You'll always be last in line for promotions and salary increases. At least for twenty years or so.]

Every employee is valuable. [We don't need duplications in Human Resources, Legal, Accounting, Marketing, Corporate Communications, Training, and many other support functions.]

We provide an environment of productivity and job satisfaction. [Please leave voluntarily. If you quit, it costs us nothing. So no more free coffee in the break room. No more holiday parties. We will ignore you. Move your office. Change your manager, your job description, the telecommuting policy—and then change it back again—until you are off-balance and dissatisfied enough to quit.]

You now have a new position… an opportunity! [A decent interval has passed and you are being quietly demoted. The new job is a dead end and might even require you to relocate. It bears no resemblance to the job you were originally hired for, and it makes no use of your best skills or experience. You can accept it or quit. You will not be supported and your performance reviews will suffer. That gives us a declining performance dossier on you, in case you sue us when we eventually fire you.]

Big companies are practical. Cutting staff makes the bottom line look better. Are their methods heartless? Demeaning? Absolutely, but they're textbook. They are only doing what big companies do—like animals in the wild. Lions don't anesthetize the wildebeests, they simply eat them. Just business.

To survive, remember these tips.

- Take charge of your own career.

- Pay attention to what the company does, not what it says.

- Reinvent yourself, be flexible and resourceful.

- Market yourself within the company, outside your original department.

- Keep looking for opportunities outside the company.

- Network, network, network.

Congratulate yourself if you survive an acquisition, but don't let it destroy you if you don't. Burn no bridges. Learn all you can and make as many contacts as possible. If you see the handwriting on the wall, put yourself in the best position to leave on your own terms—with another job lined up.

That big-name company will always look good on your résumé.

Infrequently Asked
—————————————————— Questions

D o you know why so-called frequently asked questions often fail to include the one thing you need to know? It's because they are written from the wrong point of view. I can tell you, based on insider knowledge, that many (maybe most) Frequently Asked Questions are not only not asked frequently, but they've never been asked at all.

> **Q** Does your company have Sales offices all over the world?

> **A** Why yes, we do. We have Sales offices in nineteen different countries to serve your software needs and help you find solutions, improve your efficiency and ROI, and purchase upgrades wherever you might happen to be...
> *[continues for three paragraphs]*

That's what they want you to know, not what anyone has ever asked them. A really useful FAQ is more like this:

Q All of your instructions say to click the CREATE button, but there isn't a CREATE button on the screen. How do I complete the process?

A Oh! Ha ha! Silly us. In the newest release, the CREATE button is now called the EXPORT button. I guess no one told the people who wrote the User Guide. Our bad.

But they aren't going to say that in the FAQ. It makes them look incompetent.

You might find yourself responsible for compiling an FAQ about anything—a Cub Scout event, a community ordinance, or a major new product release. So, in the interest of frustrated FAQ readers everywhere, read on...

1. Put yourself in the reader's shoes.

2. Try to use the product or service, go through the registration process, try to sign up or purchase something, whatever simulates the user experience.

3. Do a beta test with someone who knows nothing about the subject.

4. If beta testers are confused, don't roll your eyes and think, "Everybody knows that!" No, they don't. That's why they frequently ask questions.

5. Talk to actual users or read their complaints and reviews. Get feedback. Listen to it..

6. Now ask yourself, "What was not intuitive? What was confusing or difficult? What might be easily misunderstood? Was something left out? What are the next steps?"

These steps are more likely to generate helpful FAQs than trying to push an obvious agenda. So if some FAQs are no more than an un-subtle repackaging of the sales and marketing information on a website, why do they call them FAQs (Frequently Asked Questions)?

Because if they called them BSWWTSIYF (Boring Stuff We Want To Shove In Your Face), no one would read them.

—————— Voice of the Customer

B usinesses conduct surveys under the guise of communicating with their customers. They want to know what you think—what you want. This research is supposed to guide their decisions about how to serve you better.

In many cases, they respond with better products or faster service. But in others, the survey is just an excuse to do something they were going to do anyway.

It happens internally within big businesses too. For example, the champion for a multi-million-dollar software system builds a case for adopting the system. Champion conducts a needs assessment and disregards any results that don't support the cause... highlighting whatever data justifies making the purchase. Champion, of course, will oversee its installation, publicize it among the employees, and manage the system when it's adopted.

This can take two or three years. Decisions based on this kind of data manipulation seldom succeed, but by the time they fail, the champion has moved on to another project. It's called a solution in search of a problem. In huge companies, some people remain employed for years by doing this over and over.

I once worked for a small company that hired a PR firm to enhance its image. The PR group conducted a customer survey ("What is most important to you?") and announced that a new set of company goals would be the result. Customers said our products were unreliable, costly, and inferior to competitors' products. But when the products failed, we gave quick turnaround on repairs.

The only thing we did well was fix things that shouldn't have broken in the first place.

The new-image campaign resulting from this survey went something like this: Great news! Customers love our repair service! It's what they like most, and it's our new number one goal! The company did nothing to improve the quality of its products and reduce the need for repair returns. Hard to believe, I know, but they went out of business. The only people who made money from the survey were the PR folks.

The Voice of the Customer is worth listening to, but too often the survey is just an excuse to twist the responses and justify a predefined outcome. This phenomenon is not limited to business. I've seen it at work in politics—I think politicians invented the technique—social groups, communities, and even churches.

Example:

Small church, limited budget. Chairman of the church board surveys the congregation on their priorities for allocating the church money. Typical suggestions include roof repairs and better salaries for the clergy. But one elderly parishioner, who refuses to use his hearing aids, complains that he cannot hear the sermons.

So the board chairman announces the survey results. The people, he says, want a new sound system. And that's how the money is spent. Can you guess what business the chairman is in? That's right—he sells sound systems.

I don't wish him any harm, but if he were struck by lightning, I'd like to think it was divine intervention.

—————————————— Humblebragging

Sometimes also called back-door bragging, the fine art of humblebragging is self-promotion disguised as a complaint. To be clear, simple self-promotion is not humblebragging. You must appear to be trying for sympathy. "Poor me, woe is me, you should be glad you're not me..."

I first became aware of this technique many years ago when I belonged, briefly, to a women's social organization whose name sounds a little like a triple-A baseball team. (Not quite the Major League, but getting there.) At their meetings, the ladies sat around and complained about problems most people don't have:

- It's impossible find a good Mercedes mechanic in this town!

- Our pool service did not show up on the right day—again!

- I simply cannot find a refrigerated facility that stores furs for the summer!

- Andrew is having the worst trouble in school! He tested out of all the AP math courses and they have nothing advanced enough for him.

Someone start a telethon for these people.

The real messages are *I have an expensive car, a pool, fur coats, or a smart kid.*

Humblebragging is one of the most transparent of self-promotion techniques, and It's hard to believe anyone in business would fall for it. But apparently they do, because the practice persists.

- I'm sooo busy because clients won't talk to anyone else. They insist on talking to me!

- Oh no—more meetings! Out of six hundred people, why was I selected to represent our department on the Presidential Task Force?

- Not another request for a media interview! I am so tired of being the go-to expert on this subject!

- I'm going to have to lock my office door. Everyone comes in here, asking for my advice!

- I haven't taken a vacation in years because they just can't spare me for two weeks!

If you're tempted to say something like this, think about how it will affect the people around you. If they are struggling to get their careers started, they will not feel sorry for you. In fact, they might want to stick out a foot and trip you the next time you walk by. And if you're struggling to get your own career started, this practice will do you no good.

Imagine announcing at a Weight Watchers meeting that you can't find clothes small enough to fit you. Or that, no matter how much chocolate you eat, you just can't seem to gain an ounce. Or that your skinny thirteen-year-old daughter keeps borrowing your jeans. Sympathy? You'd be lucky to escape with your life.

The humblebragging at the women's social group reached its pinnacle in one perfect, ridiculous example. The city's exclusive residential area, Old Fig Garden, featured a shaded boulevard and grand old homes with beautiful, mature trees. When tree rats invaded a few attics, the neighborhood fire station stocked special bait boxes for the nearby residents. The problem was unique to Old Fig, and the local newspaper encouraged residents to pick up their bait boxes.

At one ladies' group meeting, amidst the tea-sipping and complaints about Mercedes upkeep and inadequate fur storage, one woman rose above the chatter with a loud whine, "Oh dear, it's late. I have to go by the fire station to get my rat poison."

In other words, Oh yeah? Well I live in Old Fig Garden and you don't.

Rat poison. Now that's some Major League humblebragging.

Sneaky Self-congratulation

E veryone knows it's not socially acceptable to brag about your-self (unless you're Donald Trump). But I'm always amazed at how hard some people try to pretend they're not doing it.

Most people agree that it's better to let your accomplishments speak for themselves. Broadcasting your own feats or endow-ments is tacky, and it communicates more insecurity than confidence. But in case you don't care about what astute people think—and are content to fool the great unwashed masses—here are two techniques I've observed:

The "Don't I know you from somewhere?"

> When I was in high school, I attended a state-wide conference for teenagers at a big univer-sity. During one of the receptions, I observed a tall girl working the room. She repeatedly walked up to people and said:
>
> "You look so familiar. Didn't I see you at Girls' State? The National Workshop for Outstanding

Teens? Or was it the Junior Olympics volley-ball training camp? Miss Teen America finals? Oh—maybe it was the National Science Awards dinner in Washington...?"

See how easy that is? In thirty seconds you've listed the high points on your résumé to a complete stranger. Trouble is, when people hear you do it a second time they start to catch on. So the secret is to keep moving through the crowd.

The "Someone else said about me..."

Yep, my doctor says I have the physique of a twenty-five-year-old.

My high school coach says I could still probably make the majors.

When I was on jury duty, the prosecutor said I asked such good questions I should be a lawyer.

The judges at the fair always say I make the best jam in the county.

My financial adviser said I choose better investments than he does!

You see, with this technique, you're innocently quoting someone else—not bragging about yourself. Just be careful to do it sparingly or people will figure that one out too.

Even though it was a long time ago, I often wonder what ever happened to the tall high school girl with the impressive (if suspicious) résumé. I hope she eventually had a conversation like this:

> Résumé girl—You look familiar—did I see you at the State High School Debate Finals?
>
> Response—I don't remember you. Maybe I just look familiar because my picture was in all the papers when I won.

Tone of Voice

Some people use perfect grammar, but deliver a hidden message through the tone of their delivery. Men do it too, but it's usually an undercurrent that occurs between competitive women. Just as dogs can hear frequencies of sound beyond human hearing, I think women detect tones beyond the male audio spectrum.

You probably know or work with someone like this. She says something cutting or demeaning. If called on it, she immediately starts to back-pedal and says either, "I was only trying to help" or "I was only joking."

This response blames the object of the evil intent by implying that (a) the receiver can't take criticism, or (b) the receiver has no sense of humor. Wide-eyed innocent face... awkward moment. The victim becomes the focus and cannot respond without stepping right into the trap. These barbs seem to take place in the presence of other people, in meetings, even on conference calls. It's a way to put other people on the defensive and make them look weak in a discussion or debate.

Your boss is present. (If your boss is a man, he's probably oblivious to what's going on.) You don't want to jump across the table and rip her hair out. That would make you look even worse. But it's there and you know it. Only you can't say anything. To see how it works, try this exercise:

- Say this sentence as if you sincerely want to help.

    Maybe if you used this year's numbers, the graph would look better.

Now say it again as if it were preceded by the word *"Stupid..."*

- Say this sentence as if you were making a friendly comment to a good pal.

    This is only my preliminary idea—I know you could have done it better.

Now say it again as if it were followed by *"Little Miss Perfect..."*

If these sentences are printed, the words carry no tone. That's up to the reader. But when speaking them aloud, the passive-aggressive person can always retreat to the letter of the words rather than their spirit.

I once worked with someone who was fond of asking co-workers blunt, inappropriate questions. How much money do you make? Who gave you this job? What qualifies you to run this project? Often, she caught people by surprise and they answered without thinking.

But then we banded together and agreed to answer her questions with other questions. Why would you ask such a thing? Who wants to know? Are you authorized to know that? She eventually stopped with the questions.

On rare occasions, someone suggests that the passive-aggressive co-worker apologize. The apologies may use other words, but they almost always take this tone:

> "I'm sorry you're so super-sensitive."

> or

> "I'm sorry you can't take a joke."

But two can play this game. If this happens to you, just smile, look her in the eye (eye contact is important), and say...

> "That's all right. I knew exactly what you meant."

——————————————— Truth Cards

Have you ever reluctantly shopped for a greeting card? I mean for one of those occasions when you're doing it just because you have to, or because it's expected of you? When you'd really rather say something very different from the flowery sentiment on the card?

Cards are great for expressing lovely thoughts in words you might not be able to compose by yourself. They can speak for you and make you seem poetic, sensitive, and thoughtful. They can illustrate your feelings with pictures of flowers, sunsets, and adorable fuzzy baby animals.

But perhaps their greatest value is in being able to say something you can't say with a straight face, or without gagging on the words. Or inviting a punch in the face. Life does, after all, give us many different kinds of Hallmark moments.

Here are some examples, along with hand-written comments you probably should not add, even if it's what you're thinking.

- **Happy birthday to someone who never seems to age**

  If the rest of us had as many cosmetic procedures as you've had, we'd look good too.

- **Wedding congratulations to a couple meant for each other**

  Good thing you two hooked up. Seriously, who else would want either of you?

- **Happy Fiftieth Wedding Anniversary to my dear wife**

  I have such fond memories. The years of exchanging promises, road trips in the Porsche, wonderful lovemaking, romantic dinners, and exciting travel. Most of that was with other women, but still...

- **Sorry you're under the weather. Get well soon.**

  Maybe if you drank less beer, dropped seventy pounds, and got up off the sofa you might not be in such bad shape...

- **Congratulations on your new job!**

  OK, it's with the family company and you can never be fired. But—hey—you met the basic job requirement (being a vertebrate life form).

- **Thank you for the gift**

  You've obviously forgotten it's what I gave you
  for Christmas two years ago. Now I just have
  to re-gift it to someone else.

On second thought, given the insult humor in many greeting
cards nowadays, there might be a market for a line of truth
cards. Anyone know a good graphic artist?

Playing with
Words

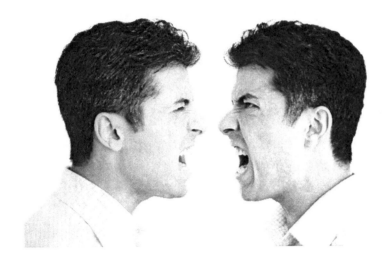

Gather a roomful of people, let them talk among themselves, and within a few minutes the word people will find each other. Word people love song lyrics, jingles, limericks, onomatopoeia, elaborate puns, and—often—crossword puzzles. It's all about how words sound, fit together in creative ways, have double meanings, and how you can play with them as if they were toys.

If you are a word person, you know it. If you're not, this section shows you why some of us laugh when the rest of the room sees nothing funny. And how some of us, when we have to wait in a long line, or the game has been rained out, or we're bored with party small talk, entertain ourselves with nothing but words.

It also shows why some of us are so critical when others use perfectly good words to make a mess of things.

——————— Useful Insult Words

D o you ever wish there were more words to describe someone so infuriating and reprehensible that ordinary in-
sults won't do? I'm not including serial killers or terror-
ists. They're in a special category of their own.

I mean the newsmakers who lie, abuse power, and squander
our money. They're on the TV news so much that the line
between real news and comedy has all but disappeared.
Some of them hold public office. Others just threaten to
run for office. Either way, they push our vocabularies to the
limit as we shout back at the TV. (Or am I the only one who
does that?)

Swear words lost their impact long ago. Relaxed obscenity
standards now allow almost anything in prime time. And if
you were interviewed on camera and stepped over a line, they
would just bleep the sound anyway.

No, it's time to revive some colorful and archaic words you
probably don't even know about. Although the origins of
these words are cloudy, they share a certain fresh nastiness

because they've not been overused. They sound like characters from a Dickens novel, but you must admit they make pretty imaginative put-downs.

- **Mumpsimus**

  Sticking to a belief or practice in the face of incontrovertible evidence that it is wrong. For example, someone who insists on ordering expresso or introducing bills declaring the earth to be flat. ("Look out the window—cornfields as far as the eye can see. Can't grow corn on a basketball!")

- **Slubberdegullion**

  A filthy, slobbering, worthless, villainous wretch.

- **Pettifogger**

  An underhanded or disreputable legal practitioner who deals with petty cases or quibbles over trifling matters.

- **Snollygoster**

  An unscrupulous person who will do anything to get elected, regardless of principles or allegiance to a platform.

You probably can't use any of these to win at Scrabble because they have too many letters. But just once, I'd like to hear a candidate in a political debate say, "What a mumpsimus! You, sir, are nothing but a slubberdegullionous, pettifogging snollygoster!"

As meanwhile, in the control room, someone asks, "So... do I bleep that or what?"

———————————— Heaven Help Us

egardless of your religious upbringing, or lack thereof,
you've undoubtedly seen names or terms rooted in various faith-based traditions used in general communication. It's impossible to know the correct spelling of every
reference from every religion, so my advice is to look before
you write.

With the resources available these days, there is no excuse for
bungling the spelling or meaning of anything.

Just remember that a major gaffe of this nature is guaranteed
to insult someone and make you look foolish at the same
time. Generally two things we'd like to avoid.

Let's hope you're not guilty of any of these.

- **Sixteenth Chapel**

   That's Sistine Chapel, in Rome. Named in
   honor of Pope Sixtus IV, not because there
   were fifteen chapels before it.

- **Twenty-third Song**

  "The Lord is my shepherd..." begins the Twenty-third Psalm. If it's the order of tunes on your iPod, never mind.

- **Pontius Pilot**

  The judge at the trial of Jesus was Pontius Pilate. To my knowledge, he was never credited with flying, steering, or guiding any kind of vessel.

- **Yon Kipper**

  First word, *Yom*, second word, *Kippur.* The Jewish day of fasting and atonement. The war named after it, in October of 1973, was not fought over smoked herring.

- **Here comes the Calvary.**

  Calvary is the site of the crucifixion of Jesus. A cavalry is a mounted fighting force, often referred to metaphorically in rescue situations.

- **Dolly Llama**

  The Dalai Lama holds a position of great honor in the Tibetan Buddhist tradition. If it's not a stuffed toy of a South American ruminant, I guess Dolly Llama is what we get for teaching our children phonics.

- **Satin-worshippers**

  Lucifer, the devil, is Satan. Satin is a shiny fabric and, unless you mean a group of deranged bridesmaids, probably the wrong word here.

If you're tempted to use any kind of religious reference, it's a good idea to follow this commandment: Thou shalt look things up.

I'm certainly no biblical scholar, but I'm pretty sure it's somewhere on the stone tablets brought down by Moses from Mount Cyanide.

Text Underlay

That's a geeky music term for the alignment of sung sylla-bles with notes in a melodic line. It involves the matchup of syllables to notes and also deals with the natural stresses of meaning and harmonic rhythm. Open vowels on long notes, properly spaced consonants, and so on.

I warned you it was geeky. But maybe it will help you explain to your children why it's not OK to repeat something just because they heard it in a song.

Vocal music often ignores the rules of grammar for the sake of text underlay. Also for the sake of authenticity (depending on the genre) or cultural effect, or just plain shock value. We can eliminate several genres from this discussion right now. Rap, hip-hop, country, reggae, rhythm and blues, heavy metal… you get the idea. Correct grammar in those songs would sound out of place. So what's left? Mainstream pop, romantic ballads, adult contemporary, anything without a cultural basis that justifies butchering the language. And that brings me to Neil Diamond.

Remember this gem?

> Songs she sang to me
> Songs she brang to me
> Words that rang in me
> Rhyme that sprang from me
> Warmed the night
> And what was right
> Became me

Brang? Really? So committed to four rhyming lines that he shoe-horned in a word that doesn't even exist? Nice text underlay but atrocious grammar. It's not the Rolling Stones (*I Can't Get No Satisfaction*), it's not Elvis (*You Ain't Nothin' but a Hound Dog*), and it's not Caribbean dialect (*Day-O*), so one wrong word sticks out. Did he think no one would notice? The lyrics are about the artist's muse and how she inspired him to write good songs. Apparently the muse was on a coffee break when he wrote this one.

Text underlay and grammar could have coexisted with something like this:

> Songs she'd sing to me
> Songs she'd bring to me
> Words that ring in me
> Rhymes that breathlessly,
> Warm the night
> And what was right
> Became me

Scoff if you will, but the best adherent to proper text underlay in modern music is Weird Al Yankovic. His parodies are classic examples of perfect text underlay, and the occasional grammatical lapses are calculated, precise, and consciously done for comedic effect. No rhymes are ever awkward or forced.

I might never forgive Neil Diamond, but I do acknowledge the need for nonstandard English in many kinds of music. In his 1957 radio show, Stan Freberg did a classic version of *Old Man River* with proper grammar as a comedy bit. "Elderly man river, that elderly man river... he must know something, but doesn't say anything..."

When Heyward and Gershwin wrote *Bess, You Is My Woman Now*, the text underlay just wouldn't have worked if someone had corrected it to *Elizabeth, You Have Officially Become My Significant Other.*

Jackalopes and Mermaids

Mermaids are, allegedly, half fish and half human. Jackalopes are half jack rabbit and half antelope. That is, cleverly constructed taxidermy evidence has convinced an amazing number of people they actually exist. Throughout the American Southwest you'll find curio shops full of picture post cards and other trinkets depicting the rabbit with antlers. As for mermaids, all I have to say is Disney.

This happens to words too, when we need a new name for something that's neither one thing or another—but both. We combined smoke and fog to create *smog*. Motor and hotel became *motel*. And who doesn't love that plastic spoon/fork doo-dad called the *spork?*

They're called portmanteau words. Many became accepted into common usage and found their way into dictionaries. But listen up, folks. That doesn't mean we can all just make them up on the spot, not even in radio ads or interviews.

1. An attorney says action will be taken summerarily.

If he's trying to combine *summarily* (at once) and *temporarily*, that makes less sense than a rabbit with antlers. It's not even a word.

2. Roofing company owner says an expert goes to the property to surmise the situation.

   Sounds like an attempt at joining *survey* with hmmm... what? *Appraise? Apprise? Advise? Analyze?* At least *surmise* (decide or assume) is a word, just not the right one for this sentence.

3. Police officer says the suspect's girlfriend was unable to co-oberate his alibi.

   Not only could she not corroborate it, she was not being corroperative.

This is a case of What Happens when inexperienced people face microphones and become tongue-tied. Consonants move around unpredictably, creating garbled syllables that sort-of-sound like real words.

So how do you prevent this from happening to you? Keep it simple. People who go all polysyllabic are more likely to lose their balance. All three of these speakers wanted to sound smart, but instead they sounded foolish.

The lawyer could have said *right away.*

The roofer could have said *size up.*

The cop could have said *confirm.*

Mermaid and jackalope words are most likely to happen in speech. But be forewarned—if you ever write one, some reader will challenge you to prove it exists. I hope you know a good taxidermist.

Flubtitles

The technology has various names, including *captioning*, *subtitles*, and *speech-to-text*. It makes video accessible to those with hearing impairments or language difficulties. But even native English speakers with good hearing sometimes use on-screen captions.

Select TV closed captioning to watch a movie while someone else sleeps. If your phone rings during the baseball game, mute the sound, turn on captions, and follow the game while continuing your conversation. Or read the subtitles with the sound on when those fast-talking actors with heavy accents are hard to understand.

Sometimes it's just plain entertaining. Screen text works best when the titles are prepared from a known script and edited before production. But with live action, neither the transcriber nor the language robot knows what's coming next. With no time to edit, that's when it happens—flubtitles.

My sympathies to anyone who truly needs subtitles to understand what's going on. With human error, autocorrect, idiomatic speech, and the hundreds of homophones in the English language, disaster is inevitable.

Screen captions often display in all-caps. I guess this avoids the question of when to capitalize and when to use lower case. Here are some of my favorites from actual TV news broadcasts (and their translations):

- GANG ACTIVITY WAS BETWEEN THE BLOODS AND THE CRYPTS

  Crips, not underground burial chambers. Although—how cool would it be if Los Angeles had catacombs like Paris!

- HE WAS TAKEN TO THE HOSPITAL AND PRONOUNCED DEBT

  They meant dead, but I guess they determined he wasn't going to pay either way.

- I WAS AGAINST THIS INVESTMENT FROM THE GECKO

  One can only hope they meant get-go, and not that insurance cartoon reptile.

So if you depend on captions to understand, and any of these appear on the TV screen, do not panic.

> BANKS WILL BE CLOSED FOR THE HOLLANDAISE

POWER NOW GENERATED BY WIND TURBANS

MAYOR SUPPORTS CITY'S RABID TRANSIT SYSTEM

Before sounding the alarm that banks are now making sauce, clean energy comes from headgear, or the trains are infected with hydrophobia, you might want to check a second source.

Marketecture

Yes, that's a word. Apparently.

I encountered it in a recent project, and something compelled me to edit it out. Certain words, even if blessed by a dictionary or Wikipedia or some credible source, are just inherently wrong.

This one, like Lord Voldemort—its name should not be spoken, is the illegitimate offspring of marketing and architecture. It means the structure of a software product from a marketing point of view. It sounds like a cheap imitation of a real word, as if the user is trying to show off. Used in a presentation, it begs the audience to ask what it means so the speaker can say, "I'm glad you asked that..." and launch into a sales pitch.

Made-up words like this are a virus in our language. Once they get started, they can become virulent. Infectious. Malignant. (Have I left out any adjectives?) There are always people who will embrace these viruses because language is a growing, evolving, changing, living thing. So are fungus and black mold.

Some will argue that language needs to adapt to changing technology, popular culture. While that is partly true, there are also people who believe that the Black Plague was a good thing because it curbed the world's population growth. But words like (you-know-what) do not adapt to anything or enrich the language. We were doing just fine without them.

Here is a warning, an example of What Happens when these viruses go unchecked. These are proposed new sub-specialties of the structure-designing business. Thanks to my favorite architect for his contributions.

- Arkitecture—homes for those who fear epic floods

- Barkitecture—kennel facilities

- Darkitecture—exclusive restaurants with sophisticated ambience

- Larkitecture—buildings designed for no good reason at all

- Narkitecture—prison cells for drug dealers

- Parkitecture—places to leave your car

- Quarkitecture—research facilities for quantum physics

- Sharkitecture—glass viewing tanks for marine museums

- Snarkitecture—houses for really snooty, unpleasant people

- Starkitecture—walled gathering places for nudist colonies

If you're groaning, it just proves my point. The challenge in effective communication is to use the words everyone knows, and use them well. If people need to understand the words you use, why make up ugly, awkward new ones?

As to Larkitecture, my architect friend says that, unfortunately, there's a lot of this. I would say the same about language desecration. And as to the language virus we discussed, consider yourself immunized.

If you still feel driven to make up words, I suggest you take up Klingon and leave English alone.

Edupreneurism

Take a deep breath. That's not really a word. At least I hope it isn't. But I did see a professional profile recently in which someone identified himself as an edupreneur.

This trend of cobbling together parts of legitimate words to make clumsy, unfamiliar new words is now officially out of control. And the trouble with these mermaid words is that they make neither good humans nor good fish.

A few years ago television started to produce docudramas, part documentary and part drama. The term *docudrama* justified dressing up the truth (the documentary part) in order to make it more interesting to watch (the drama part). Viewers remembered the drama part and catalogued it as truth in their memories.

They quoted famous characters, not realizing the lines were composed by a scriptwriter... something the character might have said, but didn't.

A similar treatment of educational subjects was called edutainment. Yep, education disguised as entertainment.

Sugar-coated education meant well, but it conditioned students to expect all learning to be effortless. It was great for toddlers with short attention spans and it tasted like candy. But eventually they had to grow up and face the broccoli. Knowledge is its own reward and it involves real work.

Russian history, neurophysiology, and getting your real estate license all have one thing in common—they don't come with animated characters or sound effects.

When you hit your audience with a word you know they won't recognize, communication comes to a halt. The invented combo-word often seeks to legitimatize something the user is trying to hide. When you combine two disparate ideas, you raise the question of which is more important. If you're an edupreneur, are you more interested in teaching me something or taking my money for an—ostensibly—educational product?

Where does it all end? For advice on building an investment portfolio, shall we go to a financitecht? To get a headshot for a print ad, do we look up an advertographer? If we're depressed but really enjoy the symphony, do we need a musichiatrist? Try looking those up in a city directory. Or stating them as your occupation on income tax returns. I guarantee you won't find them on a Career Builder drop-down list.

I've been searching for a word that describes someone who hacks off the end of one word, the beginning of another, and sticks the pieces together with duct tape. Finding none, I invented one.

That person should be called a… Lexikluge

Sounds good. I think I'll order some business cards.

Off-putting Is So...
—————————————————— Off-putting

Everyone has a pet peeve, and one of mine is the expression *off-putting*. Through-think it. The very expression describes itself. I don't know where it from-came or who up-dreamed it, but it seems the most awkward and unnecessary construction. It always sounds up-made and off-showing. At the very least, it down-slows the readability of an otherwise normal sentence.

The idea of consciously combining a verb and a preposition in reverse order would never to-occur most of us in the course of with-communicating others. If it did, we would up-foul nearly everything we tried to say. After through-plowing a few sentences of such on-goings, readers would down-shut and out-bail.

Now don't tell me it's in-listed the dictionary. I up-looked it, and I know that. But lots of egregious things have been to-added the dictionary. Like *sticktoitiveness* and *ain't*.

There's no around-getting the basic rules of grammar, although casual speech sometimes out-throws tradition in order to modernize the language. But this one seems different. Perhaps some famous statesman (or actor like-playing a statesman) once said it, triggering a massive aboard-climbing amongst the populace.

Writers with ease do it, even people with degrees do it (apologies to Cole Porter), and I about-wonder their reasons. When someone famous or prominent with-toys the language, it encourages along-going by people who should know better. It's hard to out-figure why this one up-popped.

Back in the dark ages, junior high school children about-learned the art of sentence diagramming. I suppose *off-putting*, a preposition by-followed a verb form, would be diagrammed as a hyphenated adjective. Imagine the up-giving, in-throwing of towels, and away-sneaking among twelve-year-olds as they scrambled to from-escape this one.

By now you can probably see how off-putting it is to reverse the reader's thought process by up-moving the preposition, instead of placing it after the verb where it belongs. As you read the sentence, it up-breaks the flow as if you into-fell a pothole or against-bumped an obstacle.

So congratulations if you've on-held this far without up-throwing, out-passing, or over-keeling. You are to be commended for through-muddling this turgid example. I'm sure by now you realize that I was only on-putting you for fun and I couldn't up-pass the chance to home-drive the point.

Readability matters. And, for its sake, I think we can without-do off-putting readers.

About the Author

Rebecca's corporate career spanned thirty years, first as a technical writer and editor, and then as a manager, for several companies including AT&T, FileNet, and IBM. She now lives in southern California and works independently, as Text CPR, consulting with businesses to improve their communication and training products. When not writing song parodies for the local

Rebecca Lyles

community theater, she also gives workshops and lectures on writing for both businesses and writing organizations.

http://www.textcpr.com